GREEN RECOVERY

ANDREW WINSTON

GREEN RECOVERY

GET LEAN, GET SMART, AND
EMERGE FROM THE DOWNTURN ON TOP

HARVARD BUSINESS PRESS
BOSTON, MASSACHUSETTS

ISBN: 978-1-4221-6654-3
Library-of-Congress cataloging information available.

The paper used in this publication meets the requirements of the American
National Standard for Permanence of Paper for Publications and Documents in Libraries and Archives Z39.48-1992.

The text of this book is printed using soy-based ink. The paper used for
the jacket contains 10 percent post consumer waste, and the paper used for
the text contains 30 percent post consumer waste. Both are certified by the
Forest Stewardship Council (FSC), an independent, non-governmental,
not-for-profit organization established to promote the responsible
management of the world's forests.

1 percent of the author's revenue from this book will be donated to
non-profit organizations working to create a sustainable world.

Mixed Sources
Product group from well-managed
forests, controlled sources and
recycled wood or fiber
www.fsc.org Cert no. SCS-COC-00648
© 1996 Forest Stewardship Council

**FOR THE
PLANET.**
MEMBER

Contents

Contents

Author's Note

While *Green Recovery* is fairly self-explanatory, I want to share a few thoughts about how a reader might approach this book. I also want to be transparent about my perspective and my work in this field.

First, I believe that environmental action, when done in a smart way, can create value quickly and save money fast. But of course, going green can require up-front capital at times. So I often make the distinction in the book between investments and costs. I would never say that going green is always win-win in a directly measurable way—there are often trade-offs. But investing wisely in getting leaner, smarter, and more creative will generally pay off when you include all types of value (reduced costs, lower risk, more resilient organizations, new product and service sales, greater loyalty from employees and customers, and so on). The challenges to doing this right are real, but this book, especially in the discussion on getting lean, is focused more on success stories. I'm purposely presenting an optimistic view (for pessimistic times) of how green strategy can drive business performance.

Second, I wanted to write a fairly short book with many concrete examples and ideas for moving forward quickly. These stories are not meant to be business school–length case studies. In addition, there are plenty of lists to help you focus your efforts and get started. But that said, I believe the book also provides an overall structure for deeper thinking about environmental strategy in good times and bad. In the conclusion, I provide a simple framework that shows how getting lean, smart, creative, and engaged all fit together.

Third, although many of the companies in this book are on the forefront of sustainability, they are not sustainable in everything they do, nor are they the only ones in their industries doing good work. No company is entirely sustainable—or entirely unsustainable. People can debate whether some of these companies "deserve" to be called leaders, but I know we can learn from any organization that can point to measurable, verifiable environmental and economic improvements.

Fourth, to make the book accessible and easy to read, it does not include footnotes. But I will post notes online for those who are interested in finding out more (visit www.thegreenrecovery.com or www.andrew winston.com). In the normal flow of the book, I give quick source references for quotes taken from previously published articles and studies. But much of my research was comprised of dozens of conversations with executives from a wide range of companies. Where I do not explicitly give a source, the quote came directly from those discussions.

Fifth, since I make the case in chapter 1 that transparency is a growing, powerful trend, I feel it's important to address any working relationship I have with companies covered in the book. Of the roughly 100 organizations mentioned, I have advised five companies in a consulting capacity: Boeing, Coca-Cola, Hewlett-Packard, Owens Corning, and PepsiCo. In addition, I do a great deal of speaking at industry events and corporate management meetings. I've had paid speaking engagements sponsored by thirteen organizations appearing in the book: Applied Materials, Boeing, Dairy Management Inc., Disney, Food Shippers of America, Johnson & Johnson, Procter & Gamble, SAS, SC Johnson, Southern Company, Sun, Tennant, and Xerox. Finally, periodically, I play an unpaid role in a meeting sponsored by an organization or company. From the organizations in the book, just the Carbon Disclosure Project, IBM, and Wal-Mart fit that category.

Again, this list is provided solely for transparency purposes. No companies were given any say in the content of *Green Recovery*. Of course, my relationships provided me with some access to stories and executives. I shared excerpts from the manuscript with those people I interviewed solely to check facts and allow them to confirm any quotations. But all content and conclusions drawn are my own. Where I've spoken positively about their products or services, I do not "endorse" them, but believe the environmental and economic benefits I discuss are real and provide solid lessons for other companies.

Finally, let me say a word about my intended audience. As with most business books, the target reader is any executive or manager who is looking for ideas and a deeper understanding of an important strategic issue. You may find *Green Recovery* most useful if you're relatively new to environmental issues and open to seeing the downturn as a chance to go green. But I also hope that I provide some layers of depth so that more experienced sustainability and environmental managers both find value in the framing of the discussion and also collect some good ideas for improved performance. For the sustainability executives, my real goal is to make your lives easier and help you educate your peers and managers on these issues. You can share specific parts of this story with functional managers who may find some aspects more interesting than others. For example, supply chain and logistics managers will find value in the chapter 2 discussion of fleet efficiency and the chapter 3 coverage of the strategic opportunities in gathering solid footprint data on your value chain. But I believe that businesspeople in all lines of work will find the full discussion useful for crafting new strategies and tactics.

I sincerely hope that *Green Recovery* gives you ideas that you can put to use quickly. Finally, I enjoy hearing about sustainability efforts, so please send your stories about what's working (or not) in your organizations to greenrecovery@eco-strategies.com (or twitter to @greenadvantage). Thank you for joining the conversation about how to go green and build stronger companies and a vibrant economy.

—Andrew Winston
Riverside, Connecticut
Spring 2009

GREEN RECOVERY

Introduction:
Green Recovery

Five days before he took over as CEO of the world's largest retailer in early 2009, Wal-Mart executive Mike Duke stood in front of his employees and described how different the world is today. He said it's a troubling time, with new leaders, new ideas, and a global economic crisis. Nobody, Duke said, is insulated from this situation. For the most part, his talk was what you'd expect to hear from a CEO during a recession. But then Duke went a different direction and asked the hundreds of employees in the room, and the many thousands watching online, "Sustainability is even more critical now, isn't it?"

Duke described the many environmental projects Wal-Mart remained committed to, such as reducing transportation costs and energy use across the company. To make his point as obvious as possible, he summed up, "My message to you today I hope will be real clear: we want to accelerate our efforts in sustainability, we want to broaden our efforts." This does not sound like a company slowing down its green efforts because of a recession.

So why is the CEO of a $400 billion company thinking green at a time like this? Because the smartest companies are recommitting to sustainability, and using environmental thinking not only to stay profitable, but also to drive innovation and help customers through dark times. The best organizations are preparing to emerge from the downturn better off than their competitors. To be sure, in tough times, it's hard to prioritize anything but staying alive. But survival and sustainability are truly not at odds. In fact, sustainability is at the very *core* of survival. No company, or society, can last unless it cares for all of its resources and capital—human, financial, and environmental.

Green thinking can help spur an economic recovery, both for companies and for countries. I'm not talking about the kind of recovery that moves you into the intensive care unit for twenty-four-hour support. I'm thinking more about the type of comeback that U.S. sprinter Gail

Devers made in the early 1990s. While training for the 1988 Olympics, Devers fell ill and was later diagnosed with a thyroid condition called Graves' disease. After radiation therapy, she went on to win three gold medals in the 1992 and 1996 games. In a Devers kind of recovery, you come back stronger than ever.

The hard times propel some people, and some organizations, to greatness. As *Fortune* magazine writer Geoff Colvin put it in a January 2009 article about managing in tough times,

> *It's hard to be upbeat in a recession, but it truly is an opportunity. Marathoners and Tour de France racers will tell you that a race's hardest parts, the uphill stages, are where the lead changes hands . . . When this recession ends, when the road levels off and the world seems full of promise once more, your position in the competitive pack will depend on how skillfully you manage right now.*

Green Recovery makes the case that greening your business is more important now than ever. At its core, green is about doing more with less, which can save you money quickly. It also frees up capital to invest in building a stronger, more resilient company—one ready to take the lead from slower-moving competitors.

Following the green path, *especially* in hard times, can lead your company to higher profits and sustainable advantage.

Green Is a Source of Cost Savings, Growth, and Innovation

Of all the mental hurdles keeping your company from profiting from green thinking, none compares to the misconception that environmental practices *always* cost a lot of money. But green doesn't raise costs; it lowers them (quite often in the short run, and definitely in the long run).

Although your instinct may be to retreat from green initiatives in hard times, that would be shortsighted and a huge mistake. In tight times, most companies need to focus on their bottom lines, cut costs, and conserve cash—and they need to do it fast. Reducing energy use and waste, two pillars of green, can save a great deal of money.

But as they say, nothing in life is free. If I said that environmental strategy saved money without any hard work, time, or possibly capital investment, you might think I also had a bridge to sell you. Yes, some projects will save money immediately at virtually no expense, but greater rewards often require some commitment. So if you want to reduce energy costs, asking people to turn off lights won't cost anything. But changing lightbulbs and installing motion detectors to get larger savings will clearly take some capital. The ROI will be high and the payoff fast, but it still requires some up-front expense.

So the critical distinction here is between costs and investments. Let me be blunt: if your business is unable to allocate any human or financial capital for investment—in R&D, customer relationships, people, process changes, or *anything*—then no strategy, including a green one, will matter right now. Survival will be the only priority, and that means conserving cash above all. But most companies, even in these hard times, are still making decisions about where to put their attention, people, and money every day.

For those companies that are navigating these tricky waters but also want to position themselves for dominance in the future, an environmental focus can make all the difference. Setting aside some percentage of capital expense or R&D budgets for *green* spending and innovation—as I'll show you a few leading companies are doing today—will ensure that you invest where it's most strategic.

The logic for going green is no different from the logic for pursuing other business strategies. Companies look to drive profitability, innovation, customer loyalty, employee engagement, and so on. But unlike with most other strategies, the external forces driving green thinking make this topic unique and unavoidable.

The Green Wave Rolls On

There is nothing normal about the downturn that began in 2008. Commentators have run out of ways to say that the global economic crisis is the worst in memory. The scale of the problems and the efforts to solve them are hard to grasp. If companies only had to deal with the economic situation, it would be enough.

But on top of what's unique about this moment, most of the forces driving companies to go green have not gone away. Environmental crises such as climate change and water shortages continue to evolve. Megaforces such as technology-driven transparency and the rise of the middle class in India and China—which will force the price of oil and other resources up over time—continue to advance. Closer to home, key stakeholders still demand more of companies than ever, especially corporate customers greening their supply chains. Even your employees and consumers, both of whom are under extreme financial pressure, still want some measure of environmental performance and social responsibility in the companies they work for and buy from.

All of these pressures make up an overpowering green wave that is changing business permanently. Like it or not, companies and countries must deal with current and longer-term environmental issues while simultaneously working on current economic challenges. In an open letter to President Obama during his first week in office, Stavros Dimas, the European commissioner for the environment, colorfully described the need to handle many challenges at once: "If someone's basement floods and they lose their job on the same day it is certainly an unlucky day. But they would not wait until they found a new job before pumping the basement and fixing the leak." Luckily for business, the solutions to both economic and environmental problems overlap heavily.

The same strategies and tactics that address long-term environmental challenges will help you survive today's economic conditions.

How to Recover and Get Stronger by Thinking Green

Green Recovery is a set of prescriptions for companies that want to stay healthy today and also get ready for the inevitable upturn to come. Slashing costs today frees up money to help prepare for future constraints and changing consumer demands. In tight times, figuring out what to prioritize is even more important. This book will help you focus your scarce resources on four strategic areas. You will:

- **Get lean** by revving up your energy and resource efficiency to survive the downturn.

- **Get smart** by using environmental data about products and value chains to save money, innovate, and generate competitive advantage.

- **Get creative** and rejuvenate your innovation efforts by asking heretical questions such as "Can we run our business with no fossil fuels?"

- **Get (your people) engaged** and excited by asking employees to solve their own, the company's, and even the world's environmental challenges.

Over the course of this fairly quick tour of going green in hard times, I'll show you how companies as varied as DuPont, Home Depot, and Microsoft are all getting lean. These leaders are saving tens of millions of dollars just by, among other things, filling trucks tighter, changing lightbulbs, or reducing business travel. We'll also see how Procter & Gamble got smart and used better data to launch a new laundry product that's one of a group of sustainability-themed innovations generating more than $2 billion in revenue. And we'll look closely at a revolutionary green product that's making millions for a mid-size American company that nobody would've expected to create a disruptive innovation.

The four big areas of focus will benefit your company today *and* tomorrow. Betting on efficiency and getting lean will save you money quickly, but also make you more competitive in a future with higher resource prices and more questions from customers about your environmental impacts. Gathering data on the company's environmental footprint up and down the value chain will help you identify high-priority areas for cost cutting today *and* make you smarter about where to focus longer-term innovation efforts. Getting creative means optimizing today's processes and operations *and* developing tomorrow's new products and services. And of course, the engagement and alignment of all your people makes all of these benefits possible. In short, green isn't an additional, tangential pursuit that distracts from the real work of the business; it *is* a core part of operating today.

In tight times, more than ever, the green recovery plan laid out here will make your company more competitive, no matter what its size. As you move down the green recovery path, keep in mind a few themes.

Get Lean on Stuff, Not People

Nobody could say with a straight face that layoffs are completely unavoidable. If your sales drop by 50 percent, which has happened to some automakers, you can't afford to keep everyone on the payroll. But companies may rely too much on the crutch of layoffs, which just exacerbates the recession. What's worse, many layoffs have dubious value.

A Bain & Company study from the early 2000s recession concluded that laying people off is expensive. As the study's authors reported in the April 2002 *Harvard Business Review,* if you refill a job within six to eighteen months, you lose money on the deal. The drag on earnings, they said, includes "severance packages, temporary declines in productivity or quality, and rehiring and retraining costs that more than offset the short-term wage savings."

Badly handled layoffs also destroy morale. To stay strong, to find opportunities to cut costs in smart ways, and to get creative about the future, you'll need everyone on board. So undermining morale may not be a great idea right now.

In many cases, there's another way. The money you save on energy and resource efficiency could help you avoid layoffs. At a Wal-Mart supply chain conference in Beijing in October 2008 (just as the global economy was crashing), Dave Steiner, CEO of Waste Management, spoke about sustainability in hard times. "When things are this tight," Steiner commented, "people see that it's about saving jobs and money. There's no better time to take action."

The companies that find a way to conserve cash and keep people engaged and employed will rebound the fastest when the economy turns around. So instead of relying mainly on layoffs to save money, look for resource efficiency opportunities, particularly in how you use energy.

Save Energy, Save Money

A large part of the efficiency discussion throughout this book will focus on energy. Other environmental priorities such as water, waste, and chemicals remain important long-run pressures. Reducing your footprint in those areas can absolutely save money, reduce risk, and drive innovation. But the logic for tackling energy efficiency right now is particularly compelling since the wins can be large, quick, and fall right to the bottom line—three appealing criteria when cash is tight and profits scarce.

In chapter 2, I'll share examples of companies reducing expense from building heating, cooling, and lighting; streamlining their IT operations; and slashing miles from their distribution systems. All of these activities have the potential to cut energy use 10 to 25 percent (or more). Even at a low point in the cycle of energy prices, these initiatives pay back quickly and can save you real money.

Investing in energy efficiency may be a matter of survival in the longer run as well. When fossil fuel prices rebound, the companies that are the most reliant on nonrenewable energy—either in their own business or throughout their value chains—may find the cost of operating the old, dirty way far too high for them to compete.

It may be tempting to wait until energy prices go up again before focusing on efficiency. But listen to Intuit CEO Brad Smith, who told *Fortune* magazine in January 2009 that during hard times, "you identify areas where you think you can be more efficient by assuming the worst-case scenario. Then you end up saying, Why don't we just do that anyhow?" One worst-case scenario, a rapid rise in energy prices while companies are still recovering from horrible economic conditions, could sink those on the edge. So as Smith says, just do it anyway and start getting the benefits as soon as possible. Why wait to find out—too late—that it's time to get lean?

Once you start identifying ways to reduce energy and waste, you'll start to realize that the hedge against future uncertainty is worth a great deal. As you begin to look beyond the immediate crisis, you'll see that getting lean frees up resources not only for survival, but for investment for the future.

Create a Leaner, More Innovative Culture

The same strategies that make you lean, smart, creative, and engaged to solve today's problems will help build a stronger company that can outrun its competitors. A leaner, more innovative organization will be better equipped to satisfy customers who are demanding more green products and services. You will also attract and retain the best employees who are looking for something to believe in. Given the combination of today's economic challenges and the range of green wave pressures, developing this more nimble culture may be the only way to stay alive.

Getting leaner and cutting costs frees up capital for building a greener company that can survive the ups and downs. But where should you invest today? What should you prioritize *now* to get ready for growth in better economic times? First, build the right culture for environmental thinking by investing in people and training them to understand green challenges and opportunities. Then create the space for disruptive innovation. In tight times, it's good to know that it doesn't cost anything to *think* differently or ask new, provocative questions such as "What happens to our business if oil quickly rises to $200 a barrel?"

But encouraging creativity in your employees isn't just about the future. Engaging employees pays dividends *immediately*. On a tactical level, you need their knowledge to find new, leaner ways of operating. You'll save far more money if everyone is looking for ways to cut back. On a more philosophical level, companies with a greener purpose and follow-through engage their people in a whole new way. *Is there a better time to excite people than right now, during an era of massive layoffs and rock-bottom morale?*

So imagine what your company could do with everyone pushing in the same direction, looking for ways to get lean, and thinking differently about the business.

Prepare for the Upturn and for
Long-Run Success

As in all downturns, some companies use the opportunity to focus and reinvigorate the core. Muhtar Kent, CEO of Coca-Cola, told the *Wall Street Journal* at the beginning of 2009, "Times like these are not an excuse to sit back and ride out the storm." Green efforts should be no different, especially since the forces behind the sustainability movement are not abating. Those that ignore green trends to focus solely on the travails of the moment may find themselves swept under by forces more powerful than today's economic conditions. These slow responders will miss a historic opportunity to improve their businesses.

Will green strategies *always* succeed or *always* save money quickly? Of course not. Some green initiatives—such as making products with low toxicity, sourcing organic materials, or buying renewable energy—often cost more money up front. But two essential paths in green business, using fewer resources and helping customers lower *their* environmental impacts, increase the total long-term value of the enterprise. These strategies can lower costs directly or generate new revenues, increase share, and enhance brand value. And over time, even today's lower-ROI green investments may look much better (if, for example, you redesign a product to eliminate a chemical that is then regulated or banned, or if the cost of renewable energy drops below fossil fuel prices).

This book offers a plan for a strategic green recovery based on building companies that are stronger, more environmentally sound, and more profitable. Chapter 2, *Get Lean,* will focus on five key areas of the business that hold great promise for quick wins and sizable savings: facilities, distribution, IT, telework, and waste. Chapters 3, 4, and 5—*Get Smart, Get Creative,* and *Get (Your People) Engaged*—provide critical support for getting lean and will help you position your company for future success.

There are plenty of hurdles keeping you from getting lean or getting creative—the two areas that can generate measurable, tangible value. But that's why getting smart and getting your people engaged are foundational elements of a complete green strategy. If you really know your environmental footprint and your people are committed, you can't guarantee success, but you can minimize your odds of failure. *This book presents an optimistic view of what green can do for your company in hard times.* The examples here, mainly of successful green initiatives, should help you develop your own profitable tactics and strategies.

While this book is written with a broad perspective on business for general managers of all kinds, functional experts may get more out of some pieces of the story than others. Managers in facilities, real estate, supply chain, distribution and logistics, and IT will find chapter 2 particularly useful for checking their thinking and plans against best practices. They may also look to chapter 3 for ideas on gathering and using data to drive performance. Product development and R&D might find targeted inspiration in chapter 4. Human resources and training managers in particular should consider the ideas in chapter 5. That said, managers of all stripes should find that the complete story helps them do their jobs better and think differently about how their role fits into the company's strategy.

Even in hard times, and perhaps because of them, leading companies will continue to pour the foundations for a new form of capitalism—a way of doing business that takes into account the resource constraints we face and drives innovation to build a leaner, cleaner world. Increasingly, sustainable business will become not a side issue, but a core focus of successful companies.

Going green will not only help you ride out tough times; it will help you come out of the downturn better off than your competitors. Some companies that had a weak commitment to sustainability may be pulling back now. What a great opportunity to take the lead. So get leaner, smarter, more creative, and more engaged *now* to survive, stay relevant, and prepare for a sustainable future.

Let's begin the real recovery today.

The Green Wave in Tight Times

In my previous book, *Green to Gold,* my coauthor and I describe a green wave sweeping the business world, powered by a handful of megaforces, ten environmental challenges, and twenty stakeholders asking new, tough questions. In an economic downturn, it might seem that most of these forces lose some of their power. But even today, nearly all of the fundamental reasons for going green remain intact, and many are stronger than ever before.

The environmental challenges we face as a society, from climate change and water shortages to concerns about chemical toxicity and biodiversity loss, are not going away. While at first these issues can seem alien to business strategy, think about them as constraints on resources. Traditional economic and strategy models deal with limits on labor and financial capital—in this case, we're talking about limits on *natural* capital. For example, we draw on a finite amount of clean water to live, eat, and manufacture goods. And a stable climate is a resource that we're straining.

But we're overleveraging our natural resources, much like a company overusing balance sheet assets. *To oversimplify, from an economic perspective, scarce resources get more expensive over time.* In some sense that's all that a business manager needs to understand about green. As has always been the case, the companies that get the most value out of the fewest resources profit. That's why you need to get lean and green now.

Your company may not feel environmental problems and resource constraints in the ways you might imagine (not every business relies *directly* on natural resources, but of course our entire economy does in the larger sense). Instead, you may feel pressure from critical stakeholders that care about environmental issues, from new regulation, or from megaforces such as volatile energy prices or increased demand for transparency in all that you do.

Let's look at six business drivers that are still powering a green wave, despite—and even because of—difficult economic conditions.

1. Volatile Prices for Energy and Other Resources

The historic commodity and oil price boom of 2008 was shocking and expensive for everyone. Then the world economy slowed down, and the price of oil plummeted more than 75 percent. But the downturn hides a long-term disconnect between supply and demand for most major natural resources, a mismatch that will surely raise the cost of doing business in the future.

The Supply Problem:
Not Enough at Current Prices

While cheaper energy is a boon to consumers and businesses feeling the pinch, the collapse of resource prices has had a chilling effect on supply. Industry experts worry about the slowdown in oil exploration and mining. As the *Wall Street Journal* put it in October 2008, when oil first dropped back below $80 a barrel, "Delayed or shelved exploration projects . . . could lead to a supply crimp in the next few years if and when demand comes roaring back." Six months later, in March 2009, the warnings continued as another *Journal* headline blared, "Falling Oil Supply Risks a Price Rise."

But it's not just that some projects make no economic sense at lower prices. We also face the deeper energy challenge of a worldwide plateau in oil production that some refer to as "peak oil." The contentious debate about "peak" anything aside, let's look at the actual numbers. We currently extract and use about 85 million barrels of oil per day, and the world will need 100 million barrels per day within a decade. Oil companies don't sound optimistic about reaching that goal. Here's James Mulva, CEO of ConocoPhillips, speaking to the *Wall Street Journal* in March 2008: "I don't think we are going to see supply going over 100 million barrels a day ... Where is all that going to come from?"

So, static supply is a problem. But it wouldn't matter much if we didn't need to satisfy a growing, oil-thirsty population, which brings us to the real issue ...

The Demand Problem: A Crowded World

Most statistics about China's population and economic growth are dumbfounding. Here's my favorite: China builds about 7.5 billion square feet of new space annually. To help put that number in context, imagine every single building in midtown Manhattan. Every year, China builds the equivalent of not one midtown Manhattan, but *thirty-one.*

If China's growth isn't impressive enough, add India to the mix. At a green business event in late 2008, strategist C. K. Prahalad estimated that every minute, thirty Indians move from rural areas to the city. They are looking for a better life and consuming more of everything. The rise in living standards in the developing world is one of mankind's greatest accomplishments. In his bestseller *Hot, Flat, and Crowded,* Thomas Friedman cites an Indian economist who calculated that in less than a generation, India has lifted 94 million people out of poverty—that's about "12 million more people than the entire population of Germany." Friedman's book tells a compelling tale about the megapressures driving a green revolution. The billions of new, middle-class consumers in India, China, and elsewhere are clearly the "crowded" part of the story—and they're now competing for scarce resources.

Combine this new demand with the supply challenge, and you get a volatile situation. In 2008, the daily price of oil changed 5 percent or more thirty-nine times. The weekly price changed 10 percent or more eight times versus just seven times during the previous nine years. At the end of 2008, the price of oil rose 40 percent in two weeks—and then dropped back down even faster, plummeting 12 percent in one day. You get the point.

The cost of other resources will be volatile for the foreseeable future as well. The prices of metals like copper have declined 60 percent or more from their highs. The market for recycled materials has been on a roller coaster ride. And demand for water, perhaps the most crucial natural resource, is expanding rapidly. Growing populations in dry regions place serious stress on water resources. In short, the availability and cost of *all* natural resources will remain hard to predict.

This kind of volatility is a CFO's nightmare. Under these conditions, how can you determine your cost structure? Remember, even if you're not directly reliant on resource prices, your suppliers may be. How can you make sure you've built enough margin into your prices?

But in the longer run, volatility is the lesser problem, compared to just plain high prices. The supply and demand mismatch will drive up the cost of resources. Again, the supply slowdown because of the economic recession will cause real problems when the upturn comes. As the *New York Times* reported in March 2009, "Energy experts . . . warn that oil and gas companies now cutting back on investments will be unable to respond quickly to a future economic recovery." The energy executives also sound plenty concerned about the future. As Marvin E. Odum, the vice president for exploration and production for Shell Americas, told the *New York Times* in December 2008, "We're in remission right now," but when the economy turns up, "the energy challenge will come back with a vengeance."

The downturn has one—and probably only one—positive outcome. Plummeting commodity prices give companies some breathing room to find efficiencies. Now is the time to get lean before prices skyrocket again.

2. Renewed Focus on Climate Change Regulations

The era of carbon regulation is upon us. The world's governments are in ongoing discussions about how to control emissions. The most likely outcome in most countries is a "cap-and-trade" system that sets a limit on total emissions, and then allows companies to trade for the right to pollute if they go over their individual limits.

In the United States, the Obama administration seems deadly serious about passing national legislation. During his inaugural address, Obama made it clear that climate change would rank high among the grand challenges to our prosperity, and declared, "We will work tirelessly to lessen the nuclear threat and roll back the specter of a warming planet." President Obama has assembled a green team filled with scientists and policy makers who believe sincerely in the threat of global warming and are pursuing legislation to deal with it. Early in her tenure as administrator of the Environmental Protection Agency (EPA), Lisa Jackson sent a letter to the staff telling everyone that her number one priority would be reducing greenhouse gas emissions. By March 2009, the EPA prepared to regulate carbon dioxide as a pollutant under the Clean Air Act, a major reversal from the previous administration's policies.

Things are moving quickly, but as of this writing, aggressive cap-and-trade legislation is moving through the U.S. Congress. But while the United States debates a cap-and-trade system at the *federal* level, multiple regional groups of states (and Canadian provinces) have already created their own programs. And the international community is not waiting. In 2005, Europe launched a cap-and-trade market which has had some growing pains, but it's maturing. The governments of the world are taking the threat of climate change seriously—about 190 countries sent delegations to the latest climate negotiations.

While the politicians have come to agreement on the need for action, the business community has also largely stopped debating the point. The companies most affected by carbon constraints are accepting that regulations are coming, sidling up to the table, and trying to shape the legislation to come. At an oil and gas industry conference in February 2009, CEOs discussed *which* policy, cap-and-trade or carbon tax, they preferred. The *New York Times* observed that almost all the execs "seemed reconciled to the United States' adopting some kind of climate policy."

Climate change regulations are coming and will change business forever. The attack on emissions will affect every aspect of society, from how we power our lives and travel to how businesses source, make, distribute, and sell goods. When governments and markets "price" carbon, the cost of everything changes, sometimes by a significant margin. Some products, in their current forms, will become much more expensive to make and ship (we'll explore this idea more in chapter 3).

Regardless of your beliefs about the science, your business needs to accept one immutable fact:

> **Climate change is now a political and business reality.**

The companies that get lean and less reliant on nonrenewable energy throughout their value chain will be much better prepared for a carbon-constrained world. They will also save money *now,* freeing up resources to prepare for that near future.

So it's a great time to get lean and get ahead of the curve. It's also a good time to get smart, measure your footprint, and be ready to share more information on your business than you ever imagined.

3. Greater Transparency and Openness (and the Technology to Enable It)

When you fly over coal country, you can usually see the large mining facilities where hills once stood. One of the main ways to get coal out of the ground, so-called mountaintop removal mining, leaves a large wake of destruction. One tiny environmental group, Appalachian Voices, is challenging the practices of an old-fashioned industry with a powerful modern tool: transparency.

The organization gathered publicly available information on mines and the parent corporations behind them. It then launched www.ilovemountains.org, which uses Google Earth to show anyone with a zip code a satellite view of the mountains that were destroyed to power their homes or businesses. Imagine how utilities and mining companies feel about this degree of openness.

The Internet and the technology revolution in general enable more openness than many of us are used to (or comfortable with). But some companies are getting ahead of the curve and *choosing* to release their data themselves. Following the lead of some of their natural products competitors, both Clorox and SC Johnson are posting on-line lists of every ingredient in every cleaning product they make. Patagonia, one of the most environmentally sound companies in history, has gone a step further with its "Footprint Chronicles." The Web site explores the environmental impacts of its products "from design through delivery." You can follow your sweater from a sketchpad in California, to fiber sourcing in Hungary and Japan, to assembly in China, to shipping from a distribution center in Reno, Nevada. It's too early to tell how consumers will respond to all this new openness, but it's unlikely that the share-your-innermost-thoughts Facebook and MySpace generation won't expect more of it.

The U.S. government is starting to demand more transparency as well. In March 2009, the EPA announced a new greenhouse gas tracking program that will require 13,000 power plants, factories, and other facilities to track and report their emissions. The program will cover the heavy industries responsible for a large majority of greenhouse gas emissions, and it could be in place as soon as 2010.

Clearly, transparency comes in two flavors, voluntary (Patagonia or Clorox) and involuntary (Appalachian Voices or the EPA). Guess which one is better for your business. In chapter 3 we'll look at the strategic value in gathering as much data on your environmental footprint as you can. For now, suffice it to say that your company's biggest stakeholders inside the company and out—business customers, consumers, and employees— are demanding this information anyway.

So the smart play is to gather your information and put it out there before someone else can position it for you. For those resisting this new level of openness, keep in mind one fundamental driver of the demand for transparency: the greening of the supply chain. Your customers are calling and they want answers.

4. Your Business Customers and the Greening of the Supply Chain

Let's cut right to the chase: Wal-Mart wants its suppliers to go green. And when Wal-Mart "asks" for something, 70,000 suppliers and partners listen closely.

Of course, Wal-Mart has a number of challenges (and challengers) on its path to sustainability. Many organizations have aired legitimate concerns about the company's policies on health care, labor, or pay (leading to a head-turning result in a March 2009 survey of U.S. consumers—Wal-Mart was picked as the most socially responsible company, but it also got the most votes for being the *least* socially responsible).

No matter what you think of Wal-Mart's social performance, it's nearly impossible to overstate the company's importance to the overall green movement. I spoke at a sustainability event in March 2009 and shared a panel with Duane Woods, a senior vice president at Waste Management. During his talk, Woods commented, "If we just relied on legislation, sustainability changes would be hard to drive—without Wal-Mart, much of this wouldn't be happening." So even if every other force described in this chapter ground to a halt, the greening of the supply chain in general, and the pressure from Wal-Mart specifically, would likely keep the green wave moving.

The effects are truly global. Even after this downturn was in full swing, on October 22, 2008, Wal-Mart called a meeting of Chinese manufacturers to discuss its supply chain goals. The top executives stood in front of 900 suppliers and made it clear that every company would need to meet new environmental and social standards within a few years. New demands about energy use and overall transparency were the appetizer. The main course was then-CEO Lee Scott's statement that suppliers who don't follow the path "will be banned from making products for Wal-Mart." For Chinese and other Asian suppliers that want to do business with Wal-Mart, the terms of the deal have now shifted.

As I sat watching the proceedings, I was fairly amazed at the seriousness of Scott's pronouncements. And I wasn't the only one. Peggy Liu, founder of the influential energy-focused nonprofit JUCCCE in China, turned to me and said in quiet understatement, "This is really historic, isn't it?" To put the importance of this gathering in perspective, the rumor at the meeting was that Wal-Mart is China's sixth- or seventh-largest trading partner, falling somewhere after the United States, the European Union, and Japan.

Wal-Mart has also asked some key suppliers to provide carbon footprint data on their products. Then, after some highly publicized toy recalls, Wal-Mart set its own rules about how much lead it would allow in the toys on its shelves—a standard that's 85 percent tougher than U.S. regulations. Other retailers, such as Toys "R"

Us, Target, and Sears, have phased out products with certain chemicals that studies indicate are dangerous to human health (such as BPA or phthalates).

The days when environmental "strategy" focused entirely on complying with federal or state regulations are over. When you have to abide by the toughest standards out there, and those may be from a corporate customer instead of a government, what does *compliance* even mean anymore?

So where is all this upstream pressure headed? This force is accelerating and broadening. The companies that have learned to take a value-chain perspective have discovered real value, from lower costs to superior products. They believe it's a better way of doing business. "Greening the supply chain" is now morphing from demands flowing in just one direction—from customers to suppliers—to multilateral partnerships including all the players in a full value chain. In the aviation industry, for example, engine makers (GE), plane manufacturers (Boeing), airlines (Virgin), and airports (Port of Seattle) formed a partnership to pursue "carbon-neutral growth" for the industry.

Businesses are now challenging each other to go green, in part so they can tell *their* customers and consumers all about it.

5. Your Consumers: Wanting It All

Over the last few years, with the nonstop coverage of all things environmental, you would think all consumers had become committed buyers of green products. But in these tight times, it's a fair question to ask whether they still care about environmental issues. A number of studies seem to indicate that they do.

In early 2009, Accenture released the results of a survey of 11,000 consumers in twenty-two countries. The study found that 86 percent of consumers were still concerned about climate change, and 71 percent said they would avoid buying goods that traveled long distances (up from 63 percent in 2007). Other surveys, from NPD Group and The Hartman Group, show that 50 to 75 percent of consumers seek out eco-products or consider environmental and social aspects in their purchases. Consumer actions are also changing in subtle ways that may signal shifts in values. A Natural Marketing Institute survey revealed that the percentage of Americans who regularly bring their own reusable shopping bag to stores doubled to 40 percent between 2007 and 2008.

Of course, survey results are not the same as actual purchasing behavior. As industry magazine *Retail Week* pointed out in December 2008, "While consumers may say truthfully they do still care about the environment, caring is not the same as spending." Will people pay more for green benefits, even during tough times? That may be the wrong question to ask. Instead, ask why consumers *should* pay more—why not give them everything?

When BBMG, a green-minded marketing agency, asked consumers what they look for in products, quality and price were the top two criteria. No surprise there. But three new issues beat out "convenience": where the product comes from, how energy efficient it is, and its health benefits. Consumers have become "conflicted" or "conscious" about environmental issues. They are in the process of redefining what makes a quality product to include attributes related to energy use, carbon footprint, toxicity, and origins. Are your products and services high quality in this new world?

So, increasingly, customers don't want to be forced to make a choice. The best course, while challenging to say the least, may be to satisfy conflicted consumers by designing products that create, in the words of P&G executives, "no trade-offs." Give consumers something that delivers performance and environmental benefits at no extra cost, the thinking goes, and they will beat a path to your door. Even better, prove that the greener product *saves* money (think compact fluorescent bulbs and energy-efficient appliances). The *Retail Week* article also noted that shoppers are "becoming more environmentally friendly by default, because going green can save them cash."

Here's a chance to create deeper relationships with customers in tough times by helping them go green *and* save money. But you have to be authentic or risk losing them. As *Retail Week* pointed out, "Those who lose focus on the green agenda run the risk of eroding consumer trust. If they suddenly try to pick it up again when the economic climate improves, they could lose all credibility."

In tough times, we all look for friends and advocates who are genuine. Nobody can spot whether your company is authentic better than your own employees.

6. Employees: Wanting Something to Believe In

Even in tough times, when morale is low, you still need to attract and retain the best people, perhaps more than ever. For prospective employees, in the short run, the focus may be on just getting a job. But MBA students, a vital pool of top recruits, still want meaning in their lives.

If it seems unlikely that students will worry about these issues during a recession, think again. In December 2008, after the economy had been battered for months, a *BusinessWeek* article, titled "Here Come the Millennials," said that young do-gooders were "flooding MBA programs—and bringing a keen interest in green business." At Harvard Business School, the magazine reported, "the Social Enterprise Club replaced the finance and management clubs as most popular on campus."

The economist Milton Friedman once said that "the social responsibility of business is to increase its profits" and that executives had no obligation beyond making money for shareholders. The next generation of corporate leaders is taking that narrow definition of business purpose and throwing it out the window. A March 2009 study from Net Impact and the Aspen Institute revealed that 88 percent of MBA students believe that "companies should play a role in addressing social and environmental issues." And 74 percent agree that "corporate social responsibility makes good business sense because it leads to financial profits." Your newest employees will not see a conflict between economic goals and sustainability.

The *Economist* pointed out in late 2008 that "the forces that have pushed companies to fret about sustainability . . . are not about to disappear. Nor will the desire of potential recruits to work for companies with 'values' suddenly vanish." The importance of staying focused on green during the downturn was not lost on the British magazine either. "In the competition for the best business-school graduates and other high-flyers, especially once the economy starts to recover, companies that show that they were not mere fair-weather friends of sustainability will be at an advantage."

Green-minded companies like Patagonia have long known the employee benefits of pursuing sustainability. Before the downturn, when times were very good, the company was receiving more than 1,000 résumés for every job opening, creating an incredible feeling of pride for those who make it through the gauntlet.

But as important as attracting the best may be, it's even more vital to connect to current employees. During times of low morale, engaging everyone is a challenge, but you'll need all hands on deck to ride out the storm. You'll need *everyone* engaged to find ways to get lean, to collect data and get smart, and to innovate and get creative.

While business customers, consumers, and employees are the critical three stakeholders to watch, others players are not sitting still. Non-governmental organizations (NGOs) dedicated to the green movement have not forgotten their missions. Banks are looking at environmental and climate risks more closely. Regulators are creating new laws that change how products are made and disposed of. The media outlets continue to look for "gotcha" stories that they can label "greenwashing."

The green wave rolls on. It continues to reshape how we do business, but it also moves in a new context—this truly unusual moment in time that will help propel a green recovery.

What's True *Now*: A Unique Moment in History

In late 2008, when ABC News's George Stephanopoulos asked former Federal Reserve Chairman Alan Greenspan if this was the worst economic crisis he had ever seen, he replied simply, "Oh, by far." Greenspan also said that this is "probably a once-in-a-century type of event."

No doubt we face an unusually tough economic climate. But unique times create new opportunities and new ways of thinking. The context for business is shifting fast. So before we dig into the things companies should do now to survive this downturn and prepare for the future, let's look at a few trends that are creating a new business and political environment.

New Leaders, New Ideas

Both countries and boards of directors seem to be looking for a new perspective. As the *Wall Street Journal*
reported in an article titled "CEO Firings on the Rise as
Downturn Gains Steam," in just one week in January
2009, six large publicly held companies ousted their
CEOs. Rapid turnover of top executives can bring re-
newed energy as new leaders imprint the organization
with their views.

It's an opportunity for everyone in the organization
to ask tough questions about the business. When times
were great, it was easy to avoid major change. Now, with
so much in flux, companies may be more open to disruptive ideas and heretical questions. Even veteran leaders seem to be throwing out the playbook. For proof of
some measure of the ideological chaos out there, look
no further than the CEO of Exxon announcing that he
would support a gas tax.

In the political realm, some traditional foes are, for example, agreeing on the need for green energy and jobs
programs. Look at the unexpected December 2008 op-ed
in the *New York Times* from Bob Inglis, a Republican
congressman from South Carolina, and conservative
economist Arthur Laffer. Some right-leaning politicians,
they said, were willing to consider a carbon tax, a fairly

heretical notion for fiscal conservatives. They wrote that "conservatives do not have to agree that humans are causing climate change to recognize a sensible energy solution ... when you add the national security concerns, reducing our reliance on fossil fuels becomes a no-brainer." This was more than an olive branch; it was a new path.

We're living in a time where thought leaders question, or at least adjust, some belief systems. It's an era with few sacred cows. When the situation is truly dire, people roll up their sleeves and look for allies wherever they can find them. You don't ask the political affiliation of the person handing you a sandbag to stop the floodwaters.

While it's unlikely Congress will speak with one voice, all sides of old debates seem to be rethinking their positions. With everything in flux, perhaps new ideas will get a hearing. Larry Summers, President Obama's chief economic adviser, told *Time* magazine in January 2009, "With crisis comes enormous fluidity in the system ... In Washington the transition from inconceivable to inevitable can be rapid if forced by events."

Larger Government, Giant Stimulus Packages, Big Numbers

Richard Nixon's famous quip that "we're all Keynesians now" has become very popular. Economists of all stripes are parroting John Maynard Keynes's view on fiscal policy: in recessions, increased government spending is necessary to boost the economy. Leaders around the world clearly agree and have passed massive stimulus packages. The total additional government spending totals more than $2 trillion, not even counting the trillions offered to bail out the banks.

In the United States, the scale of the numbers has changed our perspective, perhaps forever. Starting with $700 billion bailout packages, and extending to $1.5 trillion deficits, our sense of what makes for a large spending project has shifted. The press and public familiarity with large numbers shines a new light on other projects. Some big thinkers are asking, for example, why we can't power our electrical grid entirely with renewable energy. This worthy objective may cost trillions of dollars over twenty years, but perhaps we're able to imagine that scale of endeavor now. At a time when we need to think big to get out of tough times and to tackle global environmental challenges, getting more comfortable with large numbers may be a good thing.

Innovative, heretical questions are easier to pose when minds are open. Companies may now be more comfortable asking bigger, disruptive questions that can lead to serious innovation.

A Green Focus to the Stimulus

At risk of being out of date immediately, at the time of this writing, more than $100 billion of the global stimulus focuses on environmental priorities such as renewable energy, efficiency, and building more public transportation. The global total may pass $300 billion, depending on which commitments China keeps. About $80 billion of the U.S. stimulus package is going to green-tinted projects, including roughly $10 to $20 billion for each of the following:

- Tax incentives for renewable energy

- An updated or "smart" energy grid

- High-speed rail and more efficient mass transportation

- Clean water systems and other pollution reduction projects

- Improving energy efficiency in government buildings and homes

With all of this green spending, *energy efficiency is now a national and global discussion.* Government spending will stimulate demand for new technologies for energy generation and efficiency, which may impact the tools that the private sector uses to tackle these same issues. Getting lean—a central driver of corporate survival today—is now everyone's business.

A Time of Immense Change

Businesses are experiencing an unreal melting pot of forces right now: a historically unstable economy, new leadership, powerful megaforces like transparency and resource constraints, customers and employees demanding more green action, and even a global commitment to tackle something as intricate and thoroughly entwined with our lives as carbon emissions.

In total, the business world is facing a challenge unlike anything that's come before. We're in desperate need of new ways of doing business that reduce risks and costs and make our organizations stronger, more flexible, and more resilient. A green recovery can accomplish all of this and more.

Let's now explore how you can get lean, get smart, get creative, and get your people engaged during tight times.

Get Lean

You wouldn't think DuPont could find any more ways to save energy. After all, this is the company that cut greenhouse gas emissions an astonishing 72 percent over the last two decades and set an aggressive goal to hold energy use flat. Today, DuPont uses 6 percent *less* energy than it did in 1990, despite growing 40 percent. How much blood could the company squeeze from the same stone? Quite a bit, apparently.

In 2008, DuPont launched a new "Bold Energy Plan" to increase sales and lower energy use, or as management put it, "grow while shrinking." In one year, energy teams around the company found 245 new projects that cost $50 million to implement. But the initiatives also *save* $50 million every year, a short twelve-month payback. All those millions are pure profit now.

There are two big lessons here:

1. In tough times, even the leanest companies can find new ways to slash costs.

2. Green initiatives that save energy and other resources can save your company serious money that falls quickly to the bottom line.

In an uncertain economic climate, conserving cash is the first priority, and getting lean on energy and waste becomes absolutely critical. David Abney, COO of UPS, told the logistics trade magazine *Modern Materials Handling* in early 2009, "The economy is making us more hungry to conserve energy and reduce waste. It saves us real dollars if we can operate more efficiently."

When I asked Doug McMillon, CEO of Wal-Mart International, about his thinking on sustainability for hard times, he described the plan of attack this way: "It seems simple. Eliminate waste to survive and create 'capital'—human, financial, or environmental—to invest for growth." In other words, getting lean will help you ride out the hard times, preserve capital to reinvest in your people and innovation, and position you for greater profitability later.

Any "get lean" initiative should seem familiar. During hard times, all the efficiency tools you have are going to be put to the test. Whether you call it "green" or "eco-efficiency"—or by more familiar terms like total quality, lean manufacturing, and Six Sigma—doesn't matter. The green lens can lead you down some different paths than those other tools, but connects deeply to tried-and-true methods. Either way, the point is clear: use less, save money.

Some initiatives, especially those that just change behaviors, require little to no capital. These kinds of profitable opportunities are not just low-hanging fruit; they're what energy guru Amory Lovins calls "fruit on the ground"—the business equivalent of switching off the lights when you leave the room (and may literally be turning off the lights). But most projects require some modest investment.

To take a simple example, switching to an energy-efficient lightbulb may pay back in a few months, but it still requires buying a new one and installing it. Green practices can save money fast, so many are no-brainer investments. *And nearly every project described in this chapter has a payback of less than two years, and often far less.* So it's worth digging deep to find the capital you need. You're investing in building a leaner, more profitable enterprise, and, remember, *investments are not the same as costs.*

Given the tight restrictions on capital spending in most companies today, what should your priorities be? A powerful analysis from McKinsey & Company provides some clues at the macro level. McKinsey analysts looked at initiatives ranging from insulating homes to using more hybrid cars to building wind farms. They then calculated how much it would cost to reduce one ton of carbon emissions using these technologies (in consultantspeak, they drew up a "greenhouse gas abatement cost curve"). The data revealed that many of the cheapest initiatives, such as insulation and new lighting, are low tech and pay back fast.

So what can you and your organization change within months that will pay back within a year if not faster? The short answer: reduce waste in all its forms, especially energy, using many off-the-shelf technologies. Leading companies are saving significant money by changing lights, tuning up their cooling systems, shutting off computers, driving fuller trucks, and letting employees telecommute, among other things. And while initiatives in manufacturing may take longer to implement or require more capital, you can find some quick wins and inefficiencies there as well. Let's look more closely at five areas of the business where green thinking will generate savings fast.

1. Change the Lights and the Heat: Buildings and Facilities

Halifax Bank of Scotland's customers can visit more than 2,000 branches. Energy bills at the U.K. bank run about $38 million per year. So the company contracted with Schneider Electric's Buildings Division to find ways to save money and energy. The bank implemented many simple changes, such as installing more efficient lights and making sure windows were fully sealed and caulked. It also used building controls to optimize and reprogram the lighting, heating, and cooling systems to save energy. The systems turn lights off and set after-hours temperatures to warmer levels in the summer and cooler settings in the winter. Changes like these will save the bank about $1 million per year, an investment with a one-year payback.

At the same time, Schneider Electric followed its own advice and retrofitted one of its own facilities. These energy efficiency consultants surprised themselves with a 20 percent reduction in energy use and savings of $200,000, which was twice what they had estimated.

Companies can clearly find many opportunities to significantly improve building efficiency, but *two important areas offer quick paybacks: how you light space, and how you heat and cool it.* Beth Stevens, senior vice president of environmental affairs at Disney, says simply, "For quick eco-efficiency gains, lighting and HVAC are at the top of our list."

Switch to Energy-Efficient Lighting

Changing bulbs cuts costs fast. Grand Central Station in New York is saving $100,000 a year from converting to compact fluorescent (CFL) bulbs. Home Depot announced that it will save $16 million a year by changing bulbs in the in-store lighting displays. Coca-Cola Enterprises replaced 4,000 lights with a newer, high-intensity fluorescent system, which will slash energy usage by 5.6 million kilowatt-hours a year. InterContinental Hotels Group (IHG) spent $400,000 to change 250,000 bulbs and saved $1.2 million a year—a four-month payback. The examples are everywhere.

The next wave of lighting technology on the horizon seems to be light-emitting diodes (LEDs), which are already in wide use in traffic lights and little indicator lights. LEDs use much less energy than incandescent bulbs, and less energy and heat than even CFLs. They also avoid the one major downside of CFLs: the use of mercury in the bulb. The cost of LEDs continues to fall, and we'll likely see businesses switching to LEDs in the near future.

Turn Off the Lights

In a move that's both highly symbolic and profitable, Disney has begun to consistently turn off its "icons" at theme parks after hours, including the big ball at Epcot and the Tree of Life at Disney's Animal Kingdom. All castles around the world, including Cinderella's, will be put on dimmers to save energy. These giant physical brand statements have generally been lit all night, but the company has decided that it's too expensive—and the wrong thing to do—to leave them on when the parks are closed. Disney estimates that this policy shift, along with other operational changes, will save millions of kilowatt-hours. (It's an estimate because the icons are not yet on separate meters.) The move will also send a signal to millions of park "guests" that Disney is taking energy efficiency seriously, and perhaps inspire visitors to change their own behaviors when they get home.

Other companies are turning lights down or off, but in ways customers wouldn't notice. Many retailers pair skylights with software that dims the bulbs when sunlight is streaming into the building. This "daylighting" technology can slash energy use from lighting 75 percent during peak sunshine. U.K. retailer Tesco is rolling out a new green store design utilizing daylighting and other energy-efficient technologies that the company expects will cut total energy bills by 48 percent.

Update Heating and Cooling Systems

HVAC systems (short for heating, ventilation, and air-conditioning) hold so much potential for efficiency that some consultants will guarantee you savings. Semiconductor equipment maker Applied Materials hired an engineering firm to optimize its HVAC system at one of its California campuses. The firm promised a 20 percent efficiency improvement or it would forgo some fees, so the up-front risk to Applied Materials was low.

Applied will save up to $1.2 million per year, and with rebates from local utility PG&E, the payback period should be about twelve months. For obvious reasons, Bruce Klafter, Applied Materials' senior director of sustainability, says this project is "something we can sell internally to finance and other decision makers, even in tight times."

Besides saving a ton of money for companies, changing lights and HVAC systems can make a significant dent in our national energy use—roughly 40 percent of total greenhouse emissions come from buildings.

2. Cool Down or Shut Off Your Technology: IT Expense Reduction

When industry analyst Gartner Group estimated that information and communications technology was responsible for 2 percent of global carbon emissions—equal to the entire aviation industry—most people outside the IT world (and many inside it) were shocked. After all, tech companies have no smokestacks, so they seem fairly clean and green. But everyone forgot that all those computers are energy hogs. An average data center uses as much energy as 25,000 households, and info-tech use is only growing. There's a persistent and believable rumor that Google is the largest single energy user in the state of California.

Tech leaders now pitch IT solutions as the path to reducing "the other 98 percent" of emissions. The industry's approach is smart positioning, and it happens to have the added virtue of being true. Good data and technology are fundamental tools for helping companies know their environmental impacts, systematically reduce them, and find new ways to innovate (and we'll focus on these benefits in chapter 3).

But first let's take a look at IT energy use and expense and what's being done about it in three areas: (1) data centers, (2) corporate "fleets" of computers and other office technology (phones, routers, and so on), and (3) printing. Your company is surely spending far too much money powering equipment and printing documents, but the solutions are out there, and many are very cheap.

Shrink the Data Center Footprint

IT providers and users are waging a global attack on server farm design and equipment. Green Grid, a partnership founded by major tech companies such as Advanced Micro Devices (AMD), Dell, Hewlett-Packard (HP), IBM, Intel, and Microsoft, is developing new metrics and providing great information and tools for reducing a data center's footprint. The problem everyone's trying to solve is the shocking energy inefficiency of these number-crunching behemoths.

Of all the energy going into a modern server farm, IBM estimates, less than 4 percent actually processes something—you know, what the room was built for (see the figure "Energy use in data centers"). The other

Energy use in data centers

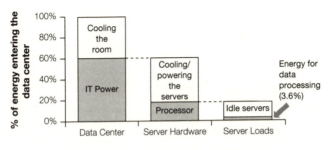

Source: IBM

96 percent of electrons cool the room itself, cool the stacks or "blades" of servers, and keep idle machines humming. Much of this energy is wasted and costs real money. In recent years, the share of a data center's variable cost going to energy has grown fast. What was once a tiny part of the budget is now 40 or 50 percent of the operating cost. Over the life of a server, you can easily spend twice as much on electricity as on the capital cost of the server itself.

The Data Center The energy problem is actually doubly wasteful: the servers generate heat (energy that's typically wasted), and then companies use more energy to pump in cool air to keep the machines from overheating. The solutions can be head-slappingly low tech. Yahoo! built a data center that uses 60 percent less energy for cooling by using a technique called *outside air economization,* which basically means opening the door and letting the hot air out. A study from Intel calculated that air cooling can cut the cost of a 10 megawatt data center by $3 million. Not surprisingly, air cooling is one of the big recommendations from Green Grid as well.

Server Hardware In keeping with a theme in this book that investments are not the same as costs . . . sometimes, as the *Wall Street Journal* suggested in February 2009, "the smartest thing to do is invest in new, more efficient systems." The paper described how Fair Isaac Corporation, which runs customer credit scores for other companies and manages a lot of data, bought new, more efficient servers and cut the total number in its data processing center in half. You should also retire old equipment that may be powered on but has outlived its usefulness. Sun Microsystems instituted a "Bring Out Your Dead" program and collected 4,100 orphaned servers. As Sun's Dean Nelson, a senior-level executive in data center design, told me, "Data centers need spring cleaning just like your house."

Server Loads Idling remains a huge problem—average server utilization hovers around just 15 to 20 percent. Older servers, when idling, can burn up to 70 percent of the power of a server running full blast. Scott McNealy, chairman and cofounder of Sun Microsystems, says, "It's like parking your car in a garage at 55 mph overnight."

Why, you might ask, are there so many servers sitting idle? Companies keep 80 to 90 percent of the server capacity idle not to waste money, but to prepare for peak volume—basically, to avoid what happened to retailer J. Crew on Inauguration Day 2009. When Michelle Obama held the Bible for her husband's swearing-in, people noticed her green gloves from J. Crew. Within a few hours, the women's section on the company's Web site was down. Then the whole site crashed, which probably cost millions in lost sales. The news media lapped up the story. As Sun's vice president of energy efficiency, Subodh Bapat, says, "If you're the IT guy, you get paid to keep the site up . . . You're always worried about your CNN moment."

Many IT providers offer highly technical solutions to this problem, such as new server designs and programming strategies. The big new buzzword is *virtualization,* which means using software to create pseudoservers that run in parallel on the same physical server and use all that idle processing power.

Addressing all three steps of the inefficiency problem can yield some impressive results. Sun consolidated one data center from 496,000 square feet to 126,000, saving millions in real estate and slashing electricity costs by $1 million annually. The consolidation in just one Colorado data center cut Sun's total global carbon emissions by 5 percent.

Microsoft's data centers use 50 percent less energy than the ones the company built just three years ago. I asked Rob Bernard, Microsoft's chief environmental strategist, to talk about how the company accomplished this feat. Bernard boils data center greening down to a few ideas: "*Look at your energy bill, do a heat scan* (to figure out where energy waste is most problematic), *improve server utilization,* and if you don't manage your own data centers, *go look at your contract.*" The last part is about the classic "landlord–tenant" problem. Providers will only have an incentive to save energy, and not just pass along costs, if customers start demanding it.

Mega IT buyers like Google and Microsoft have already started clamoring for change, and they're not alone. Tech analyst Forrester reported in January 2009 that 60 percent of IT managers are using green criteria in their procurement decisions and that even in tight times more managers are accelerating green IT efforts than slowing them down.

But what's the most powerful thing you can do to reduce IT energy use? Every time I speak to tech companies or sustainability execs, I hear one theme over and over: the people who create the energy use don't have a clue how much it's costing. The prescription:

> ## Add the power bill to the CIO's budget.

Shut Down Office Computers and Other Equipment

A single new computer may not use an excessive amount of energy—about the same as a lightbulb. But add up the millions we leave on when we're not using them, and the waste is extensive and expensive. If users of Windows Vista employed the power-saving tools embedded in the ubiquitous operating system, the United States could, according to the Natural Resources Defense Council, "cut our nation's electric bill by about $500 million per year, and prevent 3 million tons of global warming pollution."

But you don't necessarily need to *ask* all employees to put their computers into sleep mode to save money. Partners HealthCare in Boston uses software from Seattle-based Verdiem that allows the CIO to set rules about all of its 27,000 computers at once. Forcing all idle computers into standby mode, for example, can reduce energy use per PC by up to 60 percent. With this initiative, the company eliminated 5.5 million kilowatt-hours of electricity use and is saving $1.4 million a year—money that can go to patient care instead of the local utility.

It's not just computers that suck up energy. Think of all the other office equipment, like phones, routers, and printers. When these devices are connected to a network, you have an opportunity to automate them as well. Cisco recently added a feature to its network management software that allows companies to set rules for other devices. Your retail store is closed for the day? Then turn off the phones and routers. On a global level, the savings could be noticeable. According to telecommunications research company Dell'Oro Group, there are 80 million network-connected phones out there. Shutting half of them down for half the day will apparently save 800 megawatts of energy, enough to power roughly 65,000 homes instead.

The savings for an individual building or company may be modest, but every little bit helps, and automation is very cheap to implement. Keeping things powered on when nobody is around is pretty ridiculous. As our machines and networks get smarter, we can stop this wasteful practice, cut emissions, and save some money.

Cut Back on the Printers and Print Less

It's surprising how many printers one company can amass. Over time, Dow Chemical's 333 sites in 49 countries collected 16,000 printing, copying, faxing, and scanning machines. Xerox redesigned Dow's system and cut that back to just 5,500 more centrally placed devices. Fewer machines draw less energy and employees generally print less, which saves even more energy and resources upstream in the supply chain (paper production is energy intensive).

Big deal, you might say. How much could printing cost? Ursula Burns, president of Xerox, estimates that many industries spend 3 to 5 percent of revenue on content and document management. That may sound absurdly high, but reducing and centralizing machines at Dow will save the company up to $30 million in energy and materials over five years.

Granted, there were some cultural hurdles to overcome. Dow needed to get 42,000 people comfortable with the idea of walking down the hall to pick up a document. People love having their own printers in their offices. When I think about the challenge of taking away machines, I get a funny image of employees barricading their offices and, to paraphrase Charlton Heston's famous line about guns, saying that they'll only give up the printer if someone pries it from their cold, dead hands. Luckily, there's a good way to ease the transition.

Just as most CIOs don't see the cost of powering data centers, employees don't see the price of the printing services. Showing them the cost of the current system helps them get comfortable with change. But as Patty Calkins, vice president of environment for Xerox, says, "When people see how they're contributing to the *environmental* goal, it's easier to get their printers away from them. One customer felt that employees resonated with the environmental issue more than with delivering to the bottom line." In these tough times, both arguments—we'll save money and save the environment—help engage employees.

Getting leaner throughout the IT system will save a lot of cash. You can't see them, but electrons cost money. Getting leaner also means cutting back on big, physical things . . . like trucks.

3. Fill the Trucks, Drive Fewer Miles: Redesigning Distribution

Wal-Mart announced in February 2009 that it had improved the efficiency of its private fleet, one of the largest in the world, by 25 percent in just three years. To accomplish this feat, the giant retailer engaged in a range of efficiency activities, many of which—this being Wal-Mart—cost little money.

Blowing past its 25 percent goal, Wal-Mart announced it was experimenting with some new vehicle technologies, including hybrid electric power systems, trucks that use liquid natural gas, and engines that run on cooking grease from stores. In response to Wal-Mart and growing market demand in general, all the big truck manufacturers are rolling out new technologies that can improve fuel efficiency 40 percent or more. FedEx, Coca-Cola, Safeway, SC Johnson, Nike, and many others are already trying out these new models.

Technologies both old and new are reducing the footprint of cargo transportation in every mode of travel. Airlines and freight carriers are changing flight patterns and descending more smoothly to shave gallons. Cargo ships are experimenting with parachute-like sails and cushions of air (like hovercraft use) to reduce drag and improve fuel efficiency 15 to 40 percent. The shipping industry reports that fuel cells could reduce power consumption on ships in just a few years.

Reducing your distribution footprint will save money and help bolster your green claims. Even if you're outsourcing distribution, you can "look at your contract" and reduce your bills. It's been a time of rapid experimentation in how to move people and goods using as little fuel as possible ($145-a-barrel oil in 2008 helped the cause). Many of the ideas, such as keeping tire pressure up, seem small, but all together the savings add up quickly. Other steps, like investing in newer trucks, may need to wait until you've freed up enough capital for the larger investments. Here are some suggestions for best practices, ranging roughly from least expensive to most capital intensive.

Train the Drivers and Slow Down

As with most improvements, start with the cheapest option, behavior change. *Coasting, slower acceleration and deceleration,* and *avoiding pumping the gas* all improve fuel economy. At the simplest level, *slowing down* saves fuel. Office-supply chain Staples set a *maximum speed* of 60 mph for its fleet, and megashipper Con-Way Freight estimates that lowering its speed limit from just 65 to 62 mph will save the company 3.2 million gallons of fuel. At peak prices, this small change would save $15 million, or more than 20 percent of Con-Way's net income in 2008.

All trucks now come with electronic control modules that allow you to set maximum speeds, but not every company will adopt the practice. Seeking to level the playing field, the American Trucking Association (ATA) lobbied Congress in early 2009 to cap truck speeds at 65 mph. The ATA reports that driving at 75 mph uses 27 percent more fuel than moving at 65 mph. This cap, they say, could save literally billions of gallons. At first glance, restricting drivers would seem to slow down logistics. But in many cases, with fewer fill-ups, total time on the road stays flat.

Make Small, Focused Capital Improvements to the Fleet

As small as it sounds, the right *tire pressure,* or filling tires with nitrogen, can save 2 percent of fuel. *Tune-ups* and regular maintenance help as well. Wal-Mart has improved fleet efficiency 6 percent by making friction-reducing, *fuel-efficient tires* the standard on all trucks.

Changes to the aerodynamic profile of vehicles, from *side wind skirts* to *bumpers that push air down,* start to pay off big at highway speeds. A *Fortune* magazine feature in February 2009 described how the trucking conglomerate Paccar is using supercomputers to redesign everything for aerodynamics, no matter how small—tweaking the shape of tire mud flaps will save each truck $400 per year on fuel.

The low-capital ideas for getting leaner are coming out of the woodwork. Every time I speak at industry events, companies large and small approach me afterward with stories about their greening efforts. After I addressed the Food Shippers of America in March 2009, one small company told me about its "quilts" that cover pallets inside refrigerated trucks and hold the cold in. It's a solution that's a lot cheaper than buying a new, more insulated truck.

Stop Idling

Similar to data centers in IT, the biggest fuel waster in distribution is idling. Long-haul trucks spend a stunning 20 to 40 percent of their time idling, or, to put it another way, getting 0.0 miles per gallon. In milder climates, where truckers don't need as much heating or cooling when resting, educating drivers about the cost of idling (in fuel use and wear and tear on the engine) goes a long way. But to really tackle the problem, you need some relatively simple technology.

Small *auxiliary power units* (APUs) allow truckers to turn off the engine when they're sleeping or stopped for deliveries, saving more than 80 percent of the fuel wasted in idling. Wal-Mart executives say that the APU alone improved overall fleet efficiency 8 percent and, like all the other small capital improvements, paid back in less than two years.

Fill the Trucks with New Loading and Shipping Procedures

The logic is hard to fight: if you *fit more stuff on a truck,* you'll make fewer trips. Sometimes all it takes is re-designing pallets and loading practices to stack everything higher and tighter. Xerox reassigned deliveries to avoid sending big trucks when small ones would do. This "*rightsizing*" initiative, along with some other adjustments to routes, cut 21 million miles from Xerox's distribution system.

Sentinel Transportation, a joint venture between DuPont and ConocoPhillips, reduced the number of trucks leaving one DuPont site 55 percent by increasing the average payload in each truck 50 percent. For a major automotive customer, Sentinel cut distribution fuel costs in half, a much needed shot in the arm for a struggling industry. It accomplished this feat by sending a full truckload every two days instead of partial truck-loads separately. If your fleet is not completely in your control, follow Kellogg's lead and share truck space with other companies to send out full loads.

Tighten Up the Distribution System

At the most basic level, reducing distances and trips cuts costs. Chinese shipping company Cosco redesigned its delivery system to eliminate miles and cut back from one hundred distribution centers to just forty. The company saved 23 percent on logistics costs and cut carbon dioxide emissions 15 percent.

Your distribution system may have evolved from demand patterns in the past or through inertia. It may not have been optimized to reduce miles. Using global positioning systems (GPS), companies small and large are optimizing delivery routes. UPS most famously redesigned its routes to reduce miles and make "no left turns" (because waiting to cross traffic wastes time, money, and fuel). The shipping giant saved $3 million annually. A midsize laundry service company, Mac-Gray, used *GPS and other wireless technologies* to help its 400 technicians and coin collectors be more efficient. Total miles traveled dropped 15 percent while productivity shot up 20 percent. The payback was only eighteen months.

Shortening distances, shifting some shipping to rail, and many other large-scale approaches will make your distribution system leaner. But these classic strategies have taken on a new urgency and a heavy green tint. One large book publisher is planning to take over some steps in the distribution chain to reduce inventories. The goal is to replenish more quickly and print only based on demand. This plan should greatly reduce returns to the publisher, a big, expensive problem in the book business (the issue here is inventory control between the stores and the publisher, not the minor nuisance of consumers returning books). The initiative will require significant investment, but executives are moving in this direction because of the high profit potential. Reducing returns to zero would *double* the company's profitability.

But the plan also has some significant green benefits. It will reduce the miles traveled, the fuel used, and the books printed. Since paper production is energy and resource intensive, printing less will reduce the company's life-cycle carbon footprint dramatically. The sustainability executive told me that the distribution managers are driving this initiative, so it's not *technically* a green project. But, he says, "It's actually the greenest thing we're doing."

Of all the options for reducing the distribution footprint, the fastest payoffs will be changing driver behavior, setting maximum speeds, installing simple aerodynamic improvements like wind skirts, and investing in auxiliary power units. Other innovations from different parts of the business, particularly in packaging, will have large-scale impacts on shipping costs as well.

In short, the opportunities for making fleets more efficient are vast. For proof, look no further than the EPA SmartWay program and Web site, the ultimate repository of tools, stories, and advice on how to get lean in transportation. SmartWay reports that its 1,100 member companies are already saving 620 million gallons of diesel per year.

The bottom line is this: leading companies are proving that it's possible to improve fleet efficiency 25 percent or more using readily available technologies and techniques. If all private and public sector fleets achieved the same level of improvement, the United States could slash 100 million tons of greenhouse gas emissions and save some 10 billion gallons of fuel. The country as a whole would save—depending on diesel prices, which have ranged from $2.00 to $4.50 in recent years—roughly $20 billion to $45 billion.

4. Travel Less: Telecommuting and Teleconferencing

On top of moving goods more efficiently, we can change how much people move around. It seems like a small point, but you can save your company and employees a ton of money by enabling and allowing remote work.

Encourage Telecommuting

Sun Microsystems has become the poster child for flexible working arrangements. More than half of Sun's employees have no assigned desk, and nearly 19,000 telework at least part-time. Due in large part to enabling a more mobile workforce, the company downsized its office space 15 percent in 2007, avoiding $64 *million* in real estate costs. A study of Sun's home-based employees revealed that they were working three more hours per week than their regular coworkers (so much for work-life balance). The total energy footprint for those employees was down more than 5,000 kilowatt-hours per year. Employees were happier as well, since they saved two weeks of commute time per year and $1,700 in gas and wear and tear on their cars.

If we scale these benefits up to the economy as a whole, we'll see some staggering numbers. By some estimates, about 40 percent of American workers could work at home half of the time. Kate Lister, coauthor of *Undress for Success,* a book about telework, says that if we moved those 50 million workers out of the office, "we'd save 450 million barrels of oil (almost 60% of our Gulf imports), the equivalent of taking 15 million cars off the road. If just a quarter of the traditional offices were 'lights out' while the e-Workers were at home, the energy saved would power 822,000 homes."

Sun and other companies have proved that the savings are real. So consider having some of your employees work from home a few days a week. The cultural shift at the company could take some time to get used to. But in these tight times, where layoffs are all too common, imagine telling employees that you're doing everything you can to keep them but they need to work from home more. Buy-in would be high.

Reduce Corporate Travel and Meet Virtually

Companies are taking a hard look at corporate travel, particularly in service businesses where it's often the largest part of the company's carbon footprint. While you shouldn't forgo critical face-to-face meetings with customers, you can experiment with reducing internal travel. When David Ratcliffe, CEO of electric utility Southern Company, talked to the *Wall Street Journal* in early 2009 about ways to cut costs in the downturn, he mentioned two items: slashing $200 million from the capital expenditure budget by delaying some work on the physical plant and "more meetings with technology instead."

A number of companies, from Cisco and HP to niche players, have developed high-end teleconferencing systems that are, frankly, beautiful. The technology has come a long way from the days of herky-jerky motion and mismatched or delayed sound. You easily forget you're in a different city or continent from coworkers. The catch remains the high up-front cost for these quarter-million-dollar conferencing rooms. But the companies that have taken the leap and bought enough systems to see a network effect are cutting travel costs substantially. Procter & Gamble installed fifty studios in twenty-six countries, cutting one thousand international flights and millions in travel expense every month. Logically, service businesses like Deloitte and Accenture are also investing heavily in this technology.

Far cheaper than room-sized systems, Web-based meeting services also save money and connect people from a distance. Microsoft saved $90 million from reduced travel by using telecommunication tools. A study conducted by the University of Bradford and the nonprofit SustainIT, both from the United Kingdom, looked at how British Telecom (BT) employees use a suite of conferencing and collaboration systems to work together. The report calculated that BT had saved, in one year, an astounding £238 million ($330 million) in avoided travel costs and time conserved.

Between telework and telepresence, we may all spend the downturn in different rooms, but we'll be saving a lot of money and preserving capital for other strategic priorities.

5. Make Waste Pay: Reduction and Recycling

One of my favorite "reduce, reuse, recycle" stories comes from a Holiday Inn in New Orleans. After an aggressive waste-reduction initiative, the hotel asked the sanitation department to pick up the dumpster every fifteen days instead of every four. When city officials said they could not change the routes (they were somewhat busy with other priorities, like rebuilding the city after Hurricane Katrina), the hotel manager started renting out empty dumpster space to neighboring companies that were being fined for overflows. Waste reduction became a source of revenue.

Or take Burt's Bees, the maker of natural lip balms and other personal care products, which set a goal of zero waste by 2020. In just two years, the company cut landfill deliveries from 29 tons per month to just 4—an 85 percent reduction, while the business grew 50 percent. The direct cost savings were moderate, maybe $50,000. "Not 'wow' dollars," says CEO John Replogle, "but waste hauling costs dropped like a stone, recycling is up four-fold, and we're getting paid for it." The recycled materials market is down right now, but Replogle adds, "When that market comes back, we'll be better positioned and we'll see dramatic improvements to the P&L as a result."

Waste reduction is a great mission for engaging employees. Ask people to track the flow and quantity of waste leaving their department or manufacturing line. Let people who ultimately cause the waste downstream—such as product designers or engineers who may not know what comes out at the other end—see the repercussions of their decisions. As dirty as it sounds, a "Dumpsterdive" day where people measure and put a value on their waste can do wonders for awareness.

Even if the total amount of money remains negligible, the benefits of creating value from waste are more than just monetary. Imagine some of your operations people discovering that a cost center can actually make money. The search for savings or profit builds a lean mind-set that can eliminate waste in all forms, be it physical, electrical, or personal (people and their skills). In tight times, we can't afford to waste any resource.

Ten Guidelines for Getting Lean

Going green in general is not easy; it takes planning and execution, like any effective strategy. But leaning your operations, a much more narrowly defined objective than greening your products and services, may be less challenging. The fruit is sitting on the ground, and many opportunities cost very little up front or pay back so fast that it's worth stretching to free up the investment capital. As you explore easy targets and quick wins, keep in mind ten guidelines.

1. **Find the "head-slappers,"** such as using outside air to cool a data center or, on the flip side, shutting out that outside air to warm a room.

One major manufacturer discovered that the big doors to the loading dock were open all day. It didn't cost much to, you know, close them. We think we're running lean, but then we discover something so obvious, we can't believe it slipped by.

2. **Don't worry about size.** Don't look down your nose at small improvements. Each area may save a modest amount, but in total, you can make a noticeable dent in cash flow and profitability. Twenty changes of 1 percent each add up. Let them.

3. **Get everyone looking** for ways to cut back, and use cross-functional teams. (We'll talk about getting people going in the next few chapters.)

4. **Change behaviors** to save money at nearly zero capital cost. When that doesn't work . . .

5. **Automate** as much as possible. Don't just ask everyone to turn off lights—use motion detectors and software.

6. **Don't reinvent the wheel.** Look to unbiased industry and government resources like Green Grid in IT or EPA's SmartWay program for

shipping. These groups are dedicated to gathering information and best practices.

7. **Find partners and service providers** who want to reduce your costs and explore guarantees or profit sharing to reduce up-front costs.

8. **Set short-term goals.** Now is a good time for aggressive, but tactical, goals. Tell everyone to cut energy use 10 percent . . . by next month.

9. **Increase recycling,** and you may turn a cost into a small profit center.

10. **Reduce costs, but don't stop investing.** If there's a retrofit with a one-year payback, find a way to do it. It makes a big difference when you dedicate money specifically for green initiatives.

This last point is the most critical. Green projects may never get the focus they deserve without some specific money dedicated to the purpose. So do one thing above all others:

> **Set aside money specifically for energy efficiency or other green priorities.**

Why? Well let's return to DuPont, which invested $50 million in energy reduction projects throughout 2008. The one-year payback was fantastic, but where did the initial money come from? The answer is simple, but powerful. The company's Bold Energy Plan set aside 1 percent of capital expenditures solely for energy-saving ideas. All projects still met the corporate hurdle rate, so there was no special dispensation besides making the money available for worthy initiatives that managers might normally overlook.

Owens Corning leverages the same tool, but to an even larger extent. The building materials manufacturer best known for its pink insulation dedicates 10 percent of all capital expenditures to energy projects. When executives set aside these funds, they unleashed a wave of creativity and short paybacks.

If there are so many quick, high-ROI projects sitting around, why aren't companies jumping on them anyway? Two big reasons. First, energy efficiency just hasn't seemed sexy. Dawn Rittenhouse, DuPont's director of sustainable development, says, "If business units can invest in growth or energy efficiency projects, it's more glamorous to go after growth." But in a downturn, saving money starts to feel a lot more exciting, doesn't it?

The second reason is the classic problem of the urgent versus the important. Most capital expenditures go to fix things that are broken. We can't help but focus on what's leaking. At Owens Corning, people were excited to move beyond those pressing concerns and get ahead of future emergencies. But as Frank O'Brien-Bernini, the company's chief sustainability officer, puts it, "It's really about redefining what 'broken' means." Think about it: something that uses more energy than it should may not feel broken with oil at $40 a barrel, but may look like a money-eating disaster at $200 a barrel. As O'Brien-Bernini and I kicked this idea around, he added, "If your car is sitting in the driveway and you're not using it, it could be because it's literally broken, or because you can't afford to fill the tank . . . which is just as good as broken."

When it comes to energy and resource efficiency, *all* companies are broken. Our economy is broken too. Besides the obvious short-term problem of credit systems grinding to a halt, at a more basic level, we rely nearly entirely on energy from fuels that damage our health or force us to send hundreds of billions of dollars to people who don't like us very much. We've taken an "energy and resources are free" path for generations and ignored the real costs. We need a new look at how we design, produce, ship, and consume things. Without getting leaner, we may find that it's too expensive to run not just the car in the driveway, but entire segments of our economy.

Part of building a leaner, greener, cleaner, healthier, and more secure economy will be redesigning our economic relationship with natural resources. It starts with companies changing their views on energy and waste. It also starts with getting leaner in some quick-win areas like our buildings, our technology, and our distribution systems. Getting lean will free up capital both for survival and for investing in the future.

But first we need to get smarter.

Get Smart

If you put an energy meter *inside* a home and show people total usage in real time, a miraculous thing happens: they use about 10 percent less energy. The simple act of placing data in front of people changes their behavior.

Some are calling this phenomenon the "Prius effect," referring to how people respond when they see real-time fuel-efficiency data while driving the popular Toyota hybrid model. As the *Washington Post* described in May 2008, the Prius effect "can change driving in startling ways, making drivers conscious of their driving habits, then adjusting them to compete for better mileage." Data makes people smarter and inspires them to make small changes to save money and energy.

Likewise, companies can use data to encourage behavior change and get lean. Give managers statistics on their energy use—and better yet, compare them to others in the company—and they'll cut back. Then try putting information into *everyone's* hands, including perhaps even customers, and throw in some collaboration tools. The group brain trust may come up with much better ideas for getting lean and getting creative than any one person.

Now is a great time to ramp up data collection efforts. The most basic environmental metrics should capture operational numbers on energy, water, other resource use, and waste. After the basics, it's important to start gathering information on full value chain, or what I call "full brand," impacts, from suppliers and distribution to customer product use and end of life. Better data on what's happening elsewhere in the chain can save money and avoid headaches. Recent high-profile recalls of toys, nuts, and some pharmaceuticals have taught many executives that health and safety surprises coming from your supply chain can damage your brand and drag down sales.

Operating your business without environmental and social metrics leaves part of your management "dashboard" blank. How well can you run your company without complete information? But don't worry—you're not that far behind if you don't have a perfect handle on your value-chain footprint, or even your direct impacts. Many large companies I know still collect energy use data for their facilities by sending e-mails around and entering the numbers into an Excel spreadsheet. Just imagine if they gathered their financial data for their auditors this way. It's prehistoric, but it's evolving quickly, with nearly every business software company competing to make this process easier for you.

But why is it so important, especially during hard times, to understand the full story of your footprint? And what can you do with good environmental data? Here are six ways that getting smart creates value: it saves money, drives improved performance, helps you prioritize, allows you to answer tough questions from customers with hard facts, supports innovation, and guides better strategic decisions. Let's explore each of these benefits.

1. Save a Ton of Money

The Prius effect—becoming more efficient because data is visible—may be cute at the personal level, but for companies, it's serious and incredibly profitable. If you make information available, mainly to the people who can effect change based on that data, you will see major efficiency improvements and cost savings—all with little to no investment.

InterContinental Hotels Group (IHG), which operates well-known brands like Holiday Inn and Crowne Plaza, is rolling out a new software program called Green Engage. The system lets hotel managers track and see their energy and resource use. Based on best practices from around the company, Green Engage then provides a list of roughly forty possible improvements, such as building and lighting retrofits. Taking into account the specifics of each hotel, the system estimates the ROI on every investment, the total carbon reduction, and even the softer brand benefits that come from pleasing green-minded guests.

After successful energy-reducing trials at 650 properties, IHG estimates that Green Engage will enable its entire network of 4,000 hotels to reduce electricity use by up to 25 percent, a total expected savings of $200 million. David Jerome, IHG's senior vice president of corporate responsibility, reports that "the hotel managers are even more interested in this than before the economic crisis because the cost savings are so dramatic."

Saving money with better information is clearly an extension of the entire "get lean" discussion. But good data on operations is what actually enables all of the great money-saving ideas from the last chapter. You can only get lean if you know how fat you are.

But I suspect that in IHG's case, eco-efficiency success is not based solely on managers having information about their own operations. It also helps that the system shows the hotel managers how they compare to others. If you want to pump up the Prius effect, just post everyone's scores.

2. Drive Performance and Internal Competition

Heineken operates 119 breweries in 65 countries, and the company captures information on electricity, gas, and water use at all of them. The data itself helps focus managers, but so does releasing that data internally, which creates fierce interbrewery competition and drives up the efficiency of the whole enterprise. Heineken enhances the data to make sure the comparisons are fair. As one engineer from a New Zealand brewery told a national energy efficiency newsletter, "You can't just make the excuse that you use more than a European brewery because they don't need so much energy for cooling—it's all been taken into account."

Heineken doesn't rely entirely on competition to create a culture of lean. Many of the breweries tie employees' annual bonuses to performance on energy goals. But even though money is a wonderful incentive, shame works really well also—because, really, what brewery manager wants to be ranked 119th?

During my research for *Green to Gold*, I asked plant managers at 3M this question: if you had to choose, would you miss your financial targets or your environmental goals? Without hesitation, they all said the financial ones and talked about internal rankings of environmental performance. They definitely did not want to be at the bottom.

Transparency about performance also promotes sharing of best practices. If you're a brewery manager with low energy performance, wouldn't you call up a manager at the top of the list and say, "Hey, how did you get so much more beer out of every kilowatt-hour?"

3. Prioritize and Focus on the *Real* Environmental Footprint

Knowing your value chain footprint can really help you focus. When you lay out where the impacts are, you may be surprised. In tight times, you do not want to be spending time and money on the wrong things.

Take the example of yogurt-maker Stonyfield Farm, a true green pioneer. Gary Hirshberg, the founder and "CE-Yo," has directed the company to look at all aspects of the business through a green lens. Hirshberg has focused special attention on packaging. Hard facts have guided many of the company's most heralded environmental decisions. Before replacing all the plastic yogurt lids with foil, managers had collected life-cycle data to compare options. This small change reduced the company's solid waste by 6 percent, water consumption by 13 percent, and energy use by 16 percent. It also saved Stonyfield $1 million per year.

Good data has led the company down some counterintuitive paths as well. If you're trying to be greener, of course you want to make everything recyclable, right? But as Hirshberg says in his book *Stirring It Up,* "95% of the ecological damage [from packaging] comes from the energy used and the toxins created in the package manufacturing and delivery process." So the company has made light-weighting (which is what it sounds like—using less material) the top priority in packaging redesign, instead of the more typically "green" choice of recyclability. Stonyfield still uses non-recyclable plastic, but 17 percent less per cup. The benefits of lighter products ripple through the distribution system, saving energy and money at every step.

Hirschberg also pictures a day in the not-too-distant future when Stonyfield will use cups made from beets or corn. Or perhaps, he suggests, every cup will carry its own nutrients, and you'll actually eat the container. But for now, based on hard numbers, Stonyfield makes tough, but smarter choices on how to reduce its footprint.

4. Answer Your Customers' Pressing Questions

The Carbon Disclosure Project (CDP) is an initiative with a simple idea: ask companies to measure and disclose the risks and opportunities associated with climate change—and then report those answers publicly. The group might normally be laughed out of the boardroom if it weren't for the members behind the organization, the world's largest financial enterprises, representing tens of trillions of dollars in assets. More than 1,500 companies, and three-quarters of the Global 500, now answer CDP's questions annually.

A new initiative is pushing even more organizations to open up. The CDP Supply Chain Project is backed by a wide range of companies, including Boeing, HP, Johnson & Johnson, Newmont Mining, PepsiCo, Unilever, and many others. Given the breadth of support, it's safe to say that supply chains for most industries fall into their web.

These companies are asking their suppliers to disclose even more information about their carbon footprints, their strategies for reductions, their ability to track emissions by category or product, and even the suppliers' engagement with *their* suppliers. These questions will propel a ripple of disclosure pressure up the chain and raise the bar on best practices. When CDP surveyed its member companies, they gave a number of reasons why they wanted this information from suppliers. Most were innocuous answers, such as "identifying opportunities for innovation and collaboration" or the number one response, "building awareness." But the second most common answer, "grouping and rating suppliers based on their capability to respond," should send shivers down executives' spines.

For most companies, their footprint lies outside their own "four walls." So they *need* to work with suppliers, and even customers, or they can't address the biggest environmental issues or find the largest savings opportunities. So why would a customer rate its suppliers on environmental performance? Well, as they gauge environmental risks and opportunities up and down the value chain, they understandably want to know who the best partners will be, for good (collaboration) and bad (elimination). Customers will eventually drop those suppliers that can't meet the new demands.

Office Depot has already experienced the benefits of answering customer questions with good green-tinted metrics. The company has long known that fulfilling small orders for customers on a next-day basis requires more delivery trips, uses more fuel, and costs more money than fulfilling large orders less frequently. The company encourages weekly or biweekly deliveries to save operational costs, but hasn't had much luck convincing customers. Lately, though, Office Depot's director of environmental strategy, Yalmaz Siddiqui, is being invited to sales calls. Big customers have questions about how to reduce the environmental footprint of their supply chains. The company's extensive data changes the nature of the conversation.

With solid information behind him, Siddiqui can tell a customer that's receiving 100,000 shipments a year that the delivery of those orders results in an estimated

540,000 pounds of carbon emissions. Because of this environmental data and the promise of lower emissions, Office Depot has persuaded some large customers to make the switch from next-day to biweekly or even weekly deliveries. Where the operational argument failed, the environmental one opened doors. Now the customer purchasing manager can tell a green story to his management and his customers. And Office Depot demonstrates that it's a good green partner, all while avoiding significant fulfillment costs and reducing energy use and emissions.

Big corporate customers are restructuring their supply chains now, even in hard times. Many companies are quietly giving preferential treatment (such as special promotions) to suppliers with the best sustainability story. As supply chain expert and former Nike sustainability exec Phil Berry says, "We will all be evaluating our supply chain partners based on a different set of parameters." Are you ready to answer questions in this new world?

The companies that have the best data and can make a compelling case that they are the leanest will get more mindshare and shelf space. If you don't gather your data today, and fast, you may sacrifice customer relationships and sales.

5. Find Market Openings and Focus Innovation

Companies that have the best information on their entire value chain can do more than find ways to cut costs and reduce risks; they can find new market space. At Procter & Gamble, hard environmental data drove the development of an innovative product.

The company started by conducting a complete life-cycle analysis of every major product category. Looking just at the laundry segment (see figure), it's clear that the biggest energy hog in the value chain, by far, is the use of the detergent in washing machines. As Len Sauers, P&G's vice president of sustainability, told me, "We were surprised to find out what really drove our energy footprint." They were even more surprised when they realized that 85 percent of the customers' energy use came not from running the washing machines themselves, but from heating the water.

Clearly, a product that could tackle the biggest part of the footprint had potential. P&G developed and launched Tide Coldwater, which is designed to work as well in cold water as "regular" detergent does in hot water. When they use this product at lower water temperatures, consumers save money and reduce their environmental impacts. P&G considers Coldwater one of its seven "sustainable

P&G laundry products life-cycle energy use

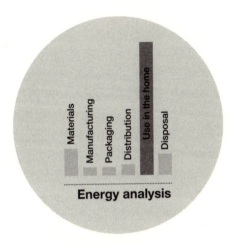

Source: Procter & Gamble.

innovation products" (SIPs), a group that generated more than $2 billion in sales in the first year. By getting smart about environmental data, P&G was able to focus innovation efforts and find the most effective ways to serve customer needs.

While P&G looked downstream to the customer's footprint, getting smarter about your upstream operations can create value as well. Cargill, one of the world's largest food companies, tracks data about agricultural commodities and uses market intelligence to stay ahead of the competition and survive hard times.

The *Wall Street Journal* reported in an article titled "Cargill's Inside View Helps It Buck Downturn" that the company's earnings stayed strong in late 2008, which demonstrated "how it uses inside information, perfectly legally, to prosper in its bread-and-butter agricultural-trading businesses." Cargill employees collect and share information about events that could influence their markets, tracking everything from shipping activities around the world to crop-disease outbreaks that affect supply. The commodity traders try to earn "small margins at each step that grain takes between producer and consumer." Cargill sometimes sells this valuable supply chain data to farmers, creating yet another source of revenue.

If Cargill understands the cost structure of every step in the value chain well enough to find margin opportunities, how hard would it be to capture environmental impacts or energy use as well (and the company may already)? Why not collect green data along with operational information?

Build a deeper understanding of your environmental impacts and costs up and down the chain, and you'll be able to focus cost-cutting and innovation efforts much better. But beyond that, you'll have the ability to make more informed strategic decisions.

6. Make Smarter Decisions and Investments

How can you best prioritize one investment over another (a core function of a good manager)? Understanding the footprint of each part of your business is a good way to start. A story from a large Canadian retailer demonstrates the role of environmental data in driving good strategy.

This retailer has mapped out its carbon and energy footprint for every store and every product on its shelves. Working with an outside software partner, Planet Metrics, the company loaded into the program measurements on energy use from every building, store, and distribution center. Then it plugged in logistics information on every shipment and product. Using macro-level data on environmental impacts across the economy to fill in some gaps (I'll come back to this in a bit), the company has assembled life-cycle data on every product line. It can now run detailed scenarios that help it make better decisions.

What if carbon is priced at $30 per ton (a reasonable estimate)? What would that do to your environmental footprint and costs for each category and product? If your business grew by 25 percent over the next five years, what would your footprint and carbon cost be? This retailer can answer these questions about the future to a very fine degree. Imagine playing a poker game where you can see all the cards. In an Old West saloon, you'd be shot for cheating the other players. Is it any wonder that this retailer has chosen to stay a bit anonymous for this story? When a company can prepare for the future much better than the competition, it doesn't want to talk about it too much.

Tyler Elm is a consulting vice president for this retailer and one of the former architects of sustainability strategies and implementation at Office Depot and Wal-Mart. Speaking about the software the company is using, Elm says, "The tool is amazing because it gives you a deep understanding of every product's footprint and lets you analyze the strategic implications of the choices you make about global sourcing, transportation, distribution, and retailing."

The product-level information on carbon intensity is the revolutionary part, and it powers new thinking. For example, when the world's governments put a price on carbon, two types of products in particular will get much more expensive to produce: (1) those relying heavily on petroleum products as inputs and (2) those with a high ratio of shipping weight to product value (think water-based items).

In the first category, Elm and his team identified products where a carbon price of $30 per ton will seriously affect the cost of goods sold (COGS). With fertilizer, for example, carbon expense will make up 35 percent of COGS. So perhaps, says Elm, the company should work with suppliers on the composition of the fertilizer and explore whether manure-based or chemical ingredients would lower costs.

In the second category, one of the retailer's highest-selling items, windshield wiper fluid, popped out of the analysis as a product that will become far less profitable once you price in carbon. The packaging has four inches of wasted space at the top, which increases shipping costs (remember, pack the trucks fuller to save energy and money). But most importantly, the entire supply chain is paying to ship something that's 90 percent water. In this case, why not ask suppliers to make a powder or concentrate that the retailer or customer can add water to?

In essence, this initiative is like the CDP supply chain group, but on steroids. With product-level data, the company can identify the specific suppliers that will cost the most to do business with and create the biggest environmental impacts. As Elm summarizes, "In a low-margin business, when carbon gets priced, wouldn't you want to know which categories will see an increase in COGS of 3 percent and which will be ten times that?"

Elm and the retailer have identified $127 million of carbon price risk in their products—very helpful knowledge for tight times. These managers can look at that risk by product and do something about it, including changing packaging, shifting where or how it's made, or redesigning the distribution system. In terms of the proverbial 80/20 rule, do you know which 20 percent of your products create 80 percent of the risk and potential cost? This retailer knows.

Now imagine having this kind of information in the business-to-business space. Business guru Ram Charan, in his recession guide *Leadership in the Era of Economic Uncertainty*, suggests that you may need to drop some customers to conserve cash. He suggests analyzing how each customer affects your business, your value chain, and your costs. But if it's OK to avoid cash-intensive customers, maybe it's time to identify resource-intensive customers and work to reduce their footprint or eliminate them. If you don't, in the near future, these customers could cost you a lot more money to keep around.

We're entering the era of what Planet Metrics' Andy Leventhal calls "carbon information management." And in good times or bad, managing your footprint data can create enormous value. Let me be clear:

> What managers can do with this environmental data represents a totally new way of running the business. This is the future of strategy.

Getting Smart in Tight Times

So what is it going to cost you to get your data together? Much less in actual capital expense than you might expect. Here are some guidelines for tight times.

"Back of the Envelope" Analysis Is OK

Even if you can't invest in large data collection systems right now, you can still get much smarter about your footprint with some limited effort. Top-line numbers on energy use from departments like IT and distribution can give you a rough sense of where cuts are most needed and valuable. Some of the information may not be readily available at first, but that doesn't mean that it's capital intensive to collect. It may just take some time and effort to dig it out.

Map Out Your Value Chain for a Quick View on Resource Use

You can start with a somewhat qualitative analysis to figure out where the biggest impacts probably are. Engage employees in the process, and bring people from different parts of the business together to map out the basic flow of the value chain. Ask yourselves some big questions (and look for opportunities to get lean and save money while you're at it):

- What comes in the door, and what did it take for suppliers to produce it?

- What do we do with our inputs, and how much energy and resources do we use?

- How much energy and resources do our customers use?

- What happens to our products after customers are done with them?

A basic life-cycle assessment can be directionally correct and give a macro perspective on the whole business.

Then you can figure out where the data gaps are and how best to estimate or fill them.

Use Data That's Already Out There

One valid complaint about gathering information from outside your four walls concerns the complexity of life-cycle analyses (LCAs). Conducting a true in-depth LCA is time-consuming and often expensive. You follow a product through every stage of its creation and get nearly exact measurements on environmental impacts at every step. Imagine how elaborate that gets for something as complicated as a computer, with hundreds of parts made from nearly every element in the periodic table.

Luckily, the resources available to help you are multiplying. Industry groups and academics have conducted LCAs on many products. You can borrow numbers from similar categories to save time and at least understand where the biggest issues lie. Let's say you produce food products, some of which have a big dairy component. The dairy industry has conducted an extensive LCA on a gallon of milk. That study can tell you that the methane produced by livestock may dominate *your* life-cycle carbon footprint as well. Or if you make an energy-consuming product, many studies (such as P&G's laundry life cycle) will tell you enough about where your footprint lies—most likely downstream in product use—to help prioritize your green innovation.

One public database in particular allows for some macro analysis. Carnegie Mellon University compiled a monster data set from government information that captures all flows of goods to and from every sector of the economy. Let's imagine you're an automaker that wants to put together an energy life-cycle footprint on your cars. The publicly available data from the smart people at Carnegie Mellon can tell you the value and quantity of all the steel sold to automakers. It also captures environmental metrics such as how much energy the steel industry uses or how much hazardous waste it produces. So you can calculate the environmental impact of each ton of steel going into cars.

Sum up all these impacts for every major element in a vehicle, and you can estimate a car's environmental footprint (on average). Multiply by production to estimate your total footprint. It's clearly not as detailed and specific as following, say, a Ford Focus from cradle to grave, but it's close enough to make strategic decisions.

The general process is called Economic Input-Output Life Cycle Assessment, or the EIO-LCA method for short. The software the Canadian retailer is using to rethink its business is based on this data. The EIO-LCA is a back-of-the-envelope calculation—on a very big envelope. The whole thing seems wonky, but it's important to know about because *the smartest companies will be using data like this to change how business is done.*

Seek Out Tools to Help You

Many software companies—from niche players like Planet Metrics to business analytics firms such as SAS to the giant tech firms—are bombarding the marketplace with tools to help you measure environmental impacts. Microsoft launched a "dashboard" for small and medium-size companies to track their energy use across the business, and Google announced "metering" software to show employees their energy use as well. A new tool from Clear Standards (now part of SAP) helps measure the ROI of different green or clean tech investments, and IBM offers similar help on assessing IT-related projects.

I can't say which products will win out. But whether you use outside tools or your own data collection and free sources may not matter at first. Either way, gather information, make sure it covers the value chain and the largest parts of your footprint, and ensure that it's direc-tionally correct.

So, in short, you can gather data at a reasonable cost. But all that said, a larger investment in getting smarter will often pay back in ways you can't imagine. Think again about the Canadian retailer that can allow for carbon regulation and future energy price fluctuations in its strategic planning. Getting this well-informed takes some effort, and a back-of-the-envelope estimate may not cut it. But look at the value you can create with a deeper commitment. This retailer has the facts it needs to make much better, more educated strategic decisions. In tough times, a company with this level of data will know where to target scarce resources to best reduce its footprint at the least cost.

The company can also focus processes and product innovation where they are most needed. This retailer understands that innovation isn't an uncontrollable process—a eureka moment in a bathtub. It can be pursued and managed. So let's turn now to how you can use innovation to prepare for the upturn to come, and emerge on top.

Get Creative

In tight times, it's extremely nice to find value in something that costs nothing. Luckily, *creativity is free*. The capital required to change mind-sets and create mental space for thinking differently is nearly nil. Some innovation may require investment, but if it's in the service of getting lean, it may pay back quickly. Even the more capital-intensive parts of innovation—actually building and testing a new product or service—may be a great investment in down times.

While it seems counterintuitive, the top minds on innovation will tell you that tough times are great for fostering creativity. Clayton Christensen, most famous for developing concepts like "disruptive" innovation or the "innovator's dilemma," told the *Wall Street Journal* in December 2008 that the economic downturn "will have an unmitigated positive effect on innovation." Cash-strapped organizations, he says, "force innovators to not waste nearly so much money."

Focusing innovation dollars where they're most needed makes sense, but that means making sure you still have *any* money for innovation. It's tempting to reduce funding to R&D to conserve cash. Don't do it—the smart companies won't. Intuit's CEO Brad Smith told *Fortune* magazine in January 2009, "We're not going to cut innovation. We're protecting the innovation pipeline so we come out of this strong." Ursula Burns, president of Xerox, told me about the dark days in the year 2000 when Xerox neared bankruptcy: "We knew that one way to improve cash position was to cut R&D. But if we did that, we'd have a near-term victory and lose the war. We'd surely mortgage our future." Today, after climbing out of that hole, two-thirds of Xerox's revenue comes from products launched in the previous two years. As Burns says, "Imagine if we had stopped—we'd certainly be less successful."

A recession is a time of great change, so you might want to wait until things go back to "normal." But what if change *is* the norm? Scott Anthony, the president of

Innosight, the firm Clayton Christensen founded, comments that "constant change is the new normal . . . things weren't all that stable to begin with." Anthony's research also shows that "many great innovations happen in recessions," including Apple launching the iPod in 2001 and IBM creating the first personal computer in the early 1980s. My father was actually one of the key executives on IBM's PC development team. He tells me that greatly lowering the cost of computing—a disruptive change that many customers needed in slower times—was exactly the point.

Today, with green pressures continuing to build, companies need products and services that use dramatically less resources. Which companies will continue to pursue these green innovations during the downturn? Will Sarni, CEO of DOMANI Consulting, comments that "those that don't really get it and view green as expendable—the dinosaurs—are slowing down their green investments." But, he says, the companies that see the true value are "the good surfers of the green wave and they aren't bailing."

Green innovation can help you take the lead in your market while others are standing still. Don't wait for environmental regulations or shifting customer demands to make your product irrelevant in the marketplace—stay ahead of the curve. For example, the governments of the world are effectively banning regular lightbulbs in favor of newer technologies such as compact fluorescents (CFLs). *You don't want to be an incandescent bulb in a CFL world.* (To push the analogy further, Professor Marian Chertow from Yale's School of Forestry and Environmental Studies points out that given the pace of innovation in lighting and the rapid development of the new LEDs, "you may not want to be a CFL much longer, either.")

Innovation in downturns is not just about survival, though. It's an essential tool for taking the lead in your industry. So bring on the seismic shifts yourself—lead the revolution, as Apple did with iTunes. The strategy guru Ram Charan lays out the opportunity in his book on leading in uncertain economic times:

> *In downturns . . . you will need to seize opportunities to make quantum leaps by focusing on new products and disruptive research. Your competitors are scared, may lack liquidity, and may be afraid of taking risks. That's a superb set of conditions for you to set up your company as a winner for decades to come.*

The kind of innovation that changes markets and turns others into dinosaurs can happen in the most surprising places—even in a seemingly sleepy industry like floor cleaning.

Tennant and Chemical-Free Cleaning

When Chris Killingstad first heard from a recruiter about a senior-level job with Tennant, a midsize Midwestern company that makes commercial floor scrubbers, he did not want to interview for the position. Even though he would be running sales, marketing, and product development for an organization with $500 million in revenues, he thought the 132-year-old company looked "totally uninteresting." At the time, Tennant called itself a "nonresidential floor maintenance equipment company," the most purely descriptive and uninspiring mission statement around.

After some nudging, Killingstad went in for a meeting, and it's a good thing. He saw a company with great potential to differentiate itself in a commodity industry. Within a few years of taking the job, Killingstad became CEO. He dedicated a portion of R&D funding for advanced research and broadened the company's mission. Now, he told employees, "we're an environmental solutions company." Killingstad asked everyone to look beyond floors and find more "environments" or surfaces to clean. The other meaning of *environmental*—safer, nontoxic, and green—was a natural addition to the mission. The broader goal unleashed creativity and led to a disruptive innovation that's shaking up the cleaning world.

Every floor scrubber on the market uses some form of chemical cleaner. Tennant's new machine, ec-H2O (pronounced *ec-water*), uses only tap water. It's a fairly simple technology that doesn't require more than basic high school chemistry to understand. The machine first adds oxygen to water. Then it uses electricity to create two streams of ions that are safe to touch, one acidic and one alkaline (or basic). The now "activated" water breaks up dirt, suspends it in the droplets, and carries it back into the machine. After about forty-five seconds, the ions recombine, and you're left with just regular water and dirt. The process makes water, as Tennant says, "behave like a general-purpose cleaner." So heavy-duty or oil-based stains will still need something stronger, but for everyday floor cleaning, it'll do the trick.

The inspiration for this new floor-cleaning technology came from an unusual place. Some R&D executives were in Japan and saw how hospitals used ionized water to clean wounds, which they had been doing for thirty years. The creative engineers thought, hey, why can't we do that on the floor? The whole innovation cycle from idea to prototype took less than eighteen months.

Because it sounds too good to be true, I spoke to one of the test customers, UNICCO, a facilities management company that provides janitorial services. UNICCO tried out the new Tennant machine in a number of malls in the Northeast. The executive in charge of those accounts told me that the device actually cleans *better* than a chemical-driven scrubber. The floor also dries faster. But what he and other customers are really excited about is that they don't have to train anyone on how to handle toxic chemicals. Even though the new machine costs more, the payback from not having to buy cleaning fluids is less than a year.

So in total, ec-H2O:

- Creates no exposure to chemicals or air pollutants.

- Requires none of the normal safety training and handling costs.

- Reduces concerns about slipping and falling since it dries faster.

- Uses 70 percent *less* water than the conventional technology.

- Saves customers money within a year.

Even with all these benefits, there is some inertia in the marketplace. It's not called "disruptive" innovation for nothing—when you put out something new, there will be skeptics. But even with some uphill battles in convincing people of the product's efficacy, Tennant's innovation, arguably the Toyota Prius of cleaning machines, is by far the most successful product launch in the company's century-plus history. As they launched it in 2008, executives hoped it would make up 10 to 15 percent of the company's floor scrubber product mix, but it quickly grabbed 20 to 25 percent internal share (and grew total market share as well). The product won the industry association's innovation award and was named a top 100 innovation of 2008 by *R&D Magazine*.

Now Tennant is expanding the product platform into other domains, licensing the patented technology to others. A handheld spray bottle is entering the commercial market, and a home version can't be too far behind.

Nobody would've remotely predicted a major innovation coming from this sector or this company. But with the right tools and incentives in place, nearly any company can create this kind of disruption. As Killingstad says, "If it can happen here, it can happen anywhere."

Tennant did many things right on the path to disruptive green innovation, from top-level leadership to focusing on how to help customers reduce *their* environmental impacts. But two themes stand out. First, the company set aside financial resources for leapfrog thinking (this should sound familiar—remember how DuPont and Owens Corning allocated funds for energy efficiency projects). Second, Tennant set aside *mental* resources, giving the R&D people leeway to think differently. Stretching your thinking does not cost anything.

So the critical element of the story was getting creative people to ask a seemingly crazy, heretical question: can we clean the floor without chemicals?

Asking Tough Questions: What's Your Heresy?

Heretical ideas have swept industries many times. If someone in the advertising, television, or music businesses had asked fifteen years ago, "What if people stop watching commercials?" or "What if everyone thinks music should be free?" they would've gotten strange looks. Then TiVo and Napster asked those questions. Of course, the latter one failed to consider some serious legal issues, but it did lay the groundwork for other (legal) business models, like iTunes. For their part, digital video recorders have forced innovation as advertisers try to replace the traditional sixty-second spot with sponsored shows and product placements.

The failure to ask big, heretical questions can sink a business or industry—the music industry is still suffering from this mistake, and sales have been down nearly every year since Napster appeared. A failure of imagination can even tank the global economy. Arguably, one major contributor to the financial meltdown was the inability of nearly everyone in that sector to ask one question: what would happen if housing prices actually *dropped* instead of rising every year? Most of the ratings agencies' financial models did not allow for a negative number in the "growth" cell. The few that did ask themselves tougher questions and largely moved out of mortgage-backed securities, such as Goldman Sachs, came through the crisis in better shape than competitors.

Even though serious economic downturns change industries and markets in profound ways, those shifts may pale in comparison to what the green wave will do to business as usual. Resource constraints and megaregulation on carbon, for example, will change how we work, play, travel, eat, and live. The time for small measures to solve environmental challenges is quickly passing. What will these pressures mean for your industry and business?

Predicting the future is difficult enough, but it's even harder when dealing with environmental challenges. Jim Butcher, the former head of Morgan Stanley's global environmental office and a scenario-planning consultant, says that we all make one serious error: "Most people think linearly, assuming next year will be a minor variation from this year. But environmental issues are often nonlinear and not gradual." How do you prepare for a tipping point change that can come upon you suddenly?

I suggest asking more radical questions. What would happen to your business—and to all the companies or consumers in your value chain—if oil were $500 per barrel? It sounds absurd, but the price of oil rose from below $20 to $145 in four years, so why not $50 to $500? Or how about asking this: what if there's no water? How would you, or your major suppliers, handle a shortage?

The megaforces—like the prospect of very expensive oil—can prompt some interesting questions. But the green lens has more value than just helping you respond to green wave pressures. It can be a powerful tool for innovation in its own right. Asking provocative questions with a green tint can unleash new ways of thinking. When times are tight and you're feeling strapped for cash, you may *need* heretical ideas that help you find completely new, and much cheaper, ways of operating *today*.

So, what's *your* heresy?

Let me share a few examples of some big-picture heresies and show how some companies are grappling with tough questions.

Can a Plane Fly with No Jet Fuel? The aviation industry is starting to ask itself this surprising question. In fact, I first heard the germ of the idea for "heretical" innovation at Boeing, a company I've advised on green strategy. In one meeting with the company's environmental executives, a few of them joked about starting a "Project Heresy" to house disruptive initiatives. Although they were kidding, I thought it was a brilliant way to help people think differently.

Boeing has run biofuel test flights with multiple airlines, including Virgin Atlantic, Japan Airlines, Air New Zealand, and Continental. The planes flew with fuels derived from various mixtures of coconut oil, the jatropha and camelina plants, and even algae. Boeing has also flown a small plane on fuel cells that the company imagines can eventually power the auxiliary equipment on jumbo jets. All these tests are a first step toward building aircraft that can fly without fossil fuels.

Nobody can predict perfectly what the costs of biofuels will be at scale, but early tests show that the yields and energy density from fuels like algae may significantly improve on jet fuel. And when fuel costs can run to more than 40 percent of your operating expense—as it did for airlines in mid-2008—isn't it worth exploring some new options?

Can We Send No Waste to the Landfill? For the employees of Subaru's facility in Lafayette, Indiana, the date May 4, 2004 holds special significance—it was the last day that anyone from the plant sent garbage to the dump. Subaru and a few other companies have reduced landfill waste not just a lot, but to zero. The automaker's program of employee engagement, incentives, and new systems for sorting *everything* is extensive, but the cost savings easily pay for all the effort. In the process, the company has slashed toxic emissions and carbon dioxide per vehicle by 55 percent and 20 percent, respectively. These benefits, and the millions of dollars Subaru saved, stemmed directly from a focus on getting lean and from asking a seemingly wacky question.

What if Cars Were a Service, Not a Product? Even with the extremely dire economic situation for automakers, it's a time of incredible innovation. For the auto industry, innovation is not just good business; it's do-or-die. All the car companies are pushing hard on new technologies, from hybrids to electrics to fuel cells. But the real heretical innovations may change the nature of car ownership entirely. Car-sharing services like Zipcar, which allow you to buy hours of car time, are still relatively small at 200,000 members, but the big rental companies are getting into the game now as well.

A different challenge to the car business comes from a highly touted start-up run by tech executive and entrepreneur Shai Agassi. Israel and Denmark have agreed to let his company, Better Place, build charging stations all over the country. Agassi's company will sell electric vehicles built by Renault-Nissan, but will maintain ownership of one core technology in the car, the battery. Drivers will pull into a station and switch out the old battery for a newly charged one. Since drivers will be renting the battery, they will effectively pay for the power and miles driven, not the battery itself.

These business models are new, but are shaking up one of the world's largest and most far-reaching industries by asking new questions. As the *New York Times* reported in a February 2009 profile, "Agassi appears to be tapping into the anything-is-possible spirit of the times . . . 'I start with the question, how do you run a country without oil?'" Apparently, Agassi is full of heretical questions.

Green marketing expert Jacquie Ottman suggests that you "ask the big question: what would it take to meet our consumers' needs with zero impact . . . or in a way that actually *restores* the environment?" And if you don't ask the deeper question about what your customers *really* need, says Bruce Klafter from Applied Materials, then "you run the risk of simply trying to build a better mousetrap rather than understanding whether your customers still need one at all." Heretical questions like these are changing industries. Which side of the transformation do you want to be on?

To be sure, innovation can cost your existing lines of business some revenue. I spoke to Xerox's Ursula Burns about the company's new ink technology, which may replace current machines. Burns posed the important question, "Will this new product cannibalize our machines?" Her quick answer was instructive: "Maybe, but someone else doing it is much worse." In short:

> **You're much better off creating a disruption than being on the other side of it.**

The problem of undermining your own successful products is the classic "innovator's dilemma," and Burns suggests embracing it. Green pressures will force this dilemma on anyone whose product or service uses more energy or resources than it could (that is, everyone).

It may be obvious, but if you want to ask heretical questions, you need some heretics. In his book *Tribes*, marketing guru Seth Godin talks extensively about how heretics are the new leaders in organizations (a big change, I'd say, from the days where the "organization man" was valued above all). As Godin says, "Suddenly, heretics, troublemakers, and change agents aren't merely thorns in our side—they are the keys to our success."

So cultivate the radical thinkers and give them some structure. Attacking your own brands requires nerves of steel. It also requires focus and an organization tuned to find these opportunities and act on them.

"Systematize" Your Green Innovation

Whether you're a big player defending your territory, or a smaller one carving out a new niche, innovation is a process you can manage and encourage. In an article he wrote for *BusinessWeek* in December 2008, innovation expert Scott Anthony highlighted some organizations that he suggested may do better than their competitors in a downturn. He described these innovation "systematizers":

> Companies that have already placed their bets on innovation can double down, creating multiyear growth gaps over their competitors. Procter & Gamble, Johnson & Johnson, General Electric, Cisco, and IBM all treat innovation like any other operating process, setting targets, measuring performance, allocating resources, and actively managing portfolios.

What's fascinating about Anthony's list of five innovators is the fact that they've all made *green* growth a strategic priority. For example, both GE and P&G have made public commitments to increase sales of more sustainable products. And IBM has launched a range of services to help build a "smarter planet," one with more energy-efficient electric grids, buildings, and transportation systems. When I asked Anthony about this correlation, he said, "It's not surprising. Those who are systematic about it will watch trends and understand how to compete not just in twelve months but in twelve years."

The companies that treat innovation like a manageable process are more versatile, more resilient in downturns, and better prepared for the future. Remember, innovation applies equally to immediate actions that make you lean today and to longer-term thinking about products and services that make you more competitive tomorrow. Making innovation systematic need not cost a great deal—it's mostly about people time and focus. So it makes even more sense in tight times.

Here are some suggestions on how to systematize green innovation.

Make It Someone's Job

Any process needs a manager. Dedicate someone now, at least partially, from the R&D or design teams to manage green innovation. You don't need to hire someone to make this role a part of someone's job. This person should work with the environmental or sustainability department—which frankly should *not* be the sole owner of green innovation since it sits outside R&D—and pursue three broad goals:

- Develop an understanding of how environmental challenges affect the company's products and value chains.

- Seek perspectives from both internal and external networks (a green advisory board can provide regular insight on the evolution of green pressures, ask heretical questions, and provide a sanity check on new ideas).

- Incorporate and drive these perspectives into the mainstream innovation process. In essence, this person will need to . . .

Build Green into Design and R&D Systems

By assessing environmental impacts throughout a product's life cycle, a Design for Environment (DFE) program focuses your creative people on the areas where they can reduce footprint the most. At Hewlett-Packard, the DFE process led the R&D group down a new path.

HP's Large Format Printing division, based in Barcelona, Spain, makes giant machines for print shops that produce everything from in-store posters to highway billboards. The solvent-based inks that these printers use can make the printing process fairly toxic. Print shops must apply for air permits and install expensive ventilation equipment to handle hazardous air pollutants.

Using its DFE process, HP developed water-based inks and a new printing technology that nearly eliminates toxicity. The nonflammable inks come in bags and boxes designed for recycling, and HP will recycle some printed material for customers as well. In total, the product and service combination creates a green offering that lowers both environmental impacts and the costs of installation and operation for customers—all of which brings HP more business. But the technology is interesting to customers for another important reason. These print shops are now feeling demand from *their* customers (it's that greening of the supply chain again). Using the new technology, one shop won a contract to print signs for the Nike Women's Marathon. The shoe giant had been looking specifically for a printer that could reduce the environmental impacts of its branding and marketing materials.

The benefits of an innovative green technology can clearly ripple forward and backward in the value chain. But this kind of disruptive innovation is much more likely to happen with a systematic DFE process in place.

Use Technology to Bring People and Perspectives Together

Bringing networks of knowledge and interest together has gotten a lot easier with social media tools (it's also inexpensive, which is good in tight times). Tech-savvy companies are harnessing people power to get as many new ideas on the table as possible. IBM conducted a large online brainstorming session with thousands of employees. As a group, they suggested that the company could apply its tech know-how to solve emerging environmental opportunities, a finding that led to IBM's "Big Green" initiative. Looking for inspiration from *outside* the company, InterContinental Hotels Group (IHG) developed an online discussion forum to pick consumers' brains about how to make a green hotel authentic.

Make Time for Green Innovation

Industrial giant 3M is a longtime innovation leader and systematizer. It's well known that the company gives technical employees 15 percent of their time to spend on any project they like. Google, the modern creativity leader, borrowed this practice and upped the figure to 20 percent—one day a week to explore ideas outside the core search and advertising business. One Google engineer told the *Harvard Business Review* in April 2008, "This isn't a matter of doing something in your spare time, but more of actively making time for it. Heck, I don't have a good 20% project yet and I need one. If I don't come up with something I'm sure it could negatively impact my review." Google also created a position, the "Director of Other," to watch and manage this innovation.

If 20 percent of your people's time sounds too expensive to bear, think about the results. How can you argue with Google's market position or with 3M's record of innovation? So why not require your creative people to spend some percentage of time on *green* innovation? Given the thorny nature of the problems and the learning curve on thinking green, you may need a dedicated focus to yield the best results.

Set Green Innovation Goals

A few years ago, GE set a goal of generating $20 billion in revenue from its self-defined ecomagination products. P&G also said in 2007 that it would sell a cumulative $20 billion of "sustainable innovation products" (SIPs), like Tide Coldwater, within five years. In March 2009, P&G bumped that goal up to $50 billion by 2012. Goals are important, but they have real meaning when you clearly define what makes some products or services greener. The P&G SIPs are "products with a significantly reduced (>10%) environmental footprint versus previous or alternative products." The reduction can come in energy, water, transportation, or material, all of which save P&G and consumers money. But it only counts toward the goal if the change reduces the *entire* life-cycle footprint by 10 percent. This interesting addition to the goal broadens thinking.

Build Scenarios, Tell Stories

Shell Oil has famously developed detailed pictures of possible futures for more than thirty years. Most companies cannot afford a dedicated think tank to run these elaborate scenarios, but they can run some simpler exercises and tell stories about the future. Scenario-planning and environmental strategy expert Jim Butcher recommends assembling a cross-functional team with breadth and diversity of experience. The scenarios could build off of some key questions, similar to the heretical questions. Butcher suggests asking, "What's the next logical crisis for our industry or business? Do environmental issues potentially affect us incrementally or in more radical, even disruptive, ways?"

Adding a green dimension makes the value chain perspective even more important. If you pose a question about resource availability ("What if there's no water?"), think about what that means for the rest of the value chain. Even if your business doesn't depend on a resource like water directly, maybe a critical supplier does. Look for weaknesses in the chain, and explore opportunities to flip the problem on its head. A start-up company called Calera developed a new cement technology that captures carbon dioxide. Calera has imagined a new scenario where the construction industry, one of the world's largest producers of carbon emissions, becomes a solution to the world's dire need to sequester carbon. So instead of spending its future paying a carbon tax, maybe the cement industry will be collecting money from a whole new set of customers. That's a powerful new story line.

Ten Ideas for Green Innovation in Tight Times

From the examples of companies like Tennant and the innovation systematizers, I draw a handful of themes and lessons.

1. **Look for innovation opportunities in *all* parts of the business.** It's easy to get caught in a mental trap where cool new innovation is all about new products. But it also takes real creativity to get lean in unsexy operational areas like facilities, IT, and distribution. Finding new ways to be eco-efficient, as 3M and DuPont have done for decades, is innovative too. So expand the

definitions of design and innovation. Imagine giving operational managers awards for good *design* if they streamline a process or save energy.

2. **Set aside money and people for the cause.** I've said plenty about setting aside funds. Remember how DuPont allocated 1 percent of capital expenditures for energy initiatives? Well, the company also made sure that people resources were dedicated to the challenge. Sustainability managers found energy champions at different sites and made the goals of the Bold Energy Plan part of their responsibilities. As Dawn Rittenhouse, DuPont's director of sustainable development, put it, "Before, it was nobody's job, and it was everybody's job . . . so we made it *some*body's job."

3. **Rethink packaging to find surprisingly big opportunities.** Packaging can create enormous footprint ripples, and not just because of the significant upstream environmental impacts of paper and plastic. When you reduce packaging, you can fit more goods on every truck and retail shelf. Some reductions, like Kellogg's recent foray into smaller cereal boxes, just eliminate air.

Other packaging changes require a product re-formulation as well. Procter & Gamble concentrated its detergents to allow for "compacted" packaging. This single product redesign allowed P&G to eliminate an impressive 40,000 truck-loads per year.

4. **Look for scalable actions and close parallels for quick wins.** Everyone knows that putting your computer in sleep mode saves power. But as we saw in chapter 2, software products now allow you to automate the process, which scales the effort up to every computer at once. Similarly, supermarkets have had doors on frozen food cases for years. Some are trying doors on *refrigerated* cases as well, cutting energy use as much as 70 percent in that aisle. In some instances, however, customers don't like the change. Although not every possible initiative will work out perfectly in a different setting, it's still a great way to experiment and stretch your thinking.

5. **"Take cues from outside the category,"** recommends social entrepreneur Jonathan Greenblatt. Broaden your perspective and look beyond close parallels to find inspiration from other

industries or academic fields. When Tennant's CEO redefined the company as an environmental solutions provider, he opened minds, which led designers to find inspiration in a Japanese hospital. As Killingstad says, "If you draw the boundaries wider, you give people the freedom to explore a different context, and the ideas will come."

For a completely different angle, look to nature and the field of "biomimicry," which was pioneered by green innovator Janine Benyus. For example, swimwear company Speedo designed the "sharksuit" that Michael Phelps and other Olympians wear by studying how a shark's skin helps it reduce drag and move through the water with amazing efficiency. Calera's carbon-sequestering cement technology mimics the formation of coral. Nature is full of bright ideas.

6. **Get your data in order, and understand the life-cycle footprint.** It's worth repeating here that you can't get creative without getting smart first. Those who understand *where* in the value chain the environmental and financial costs are greatest will think differently about solutions. Which brings us to . . .

7. **Look to reduce the customer's footprint.**
   When everyone is looking for ways to cut back, companies that help their customers reduce environmental impacts and costs can grab market share. Waste Management, which normally gets paid by the ton and would seem to want as much garbage as you can generate, also has a growing services business called Upstream. This division, fully embracing the "eat your own lunch" philosophy, helps companies reduce their total waste and even explores issues as far back in the value chain as product design. The company is trying to help customers reduce waste and make products that are more easily recycled.

   With the vast opportunities in the economy to get lean and streamline buildings and facilities, companies that specialize in those services can do very well. Johnson Controls has built a $10 billion–plus building services division that helps companies and communities get lean. Since Johnson Controls' other divisions have significant exposure to the automotive sector, the buildings business has propped up earnings in recent years.

So it's not just good business to get lean; it's *great* business to help others do it as well.

8. **Find value in unexpected places.** As the world's governments start to put a value on carbon, companies may find extra money lying around. New innovators in the energy and carbon management space, such as Verdeo Group or EKO, help companies reduce emissions or manage land assets to create carbon credits. Finding some free money for things you may already be doing is a pretty good deal. The Atrio Shopping Center in Villach, Austria, has a built-in geothermal energy system inside its "piles" (the deeply buried concrete columns that hold a building up). The physical foundation of the mall now props up earnings as well by generating energy and saving the owners money.

9. **Find competition in unexpected places.** If you look at your business through a green lens, you may find ways to compete in new spaces. Those teleconferencing systems that save companies travel costs are not competing with the phone. No, these new communication tools are now taking customers away from airlines, which

probably did not expect to be competing with tech companies. A significant part of the sales pitch for telepresence systems is the reduction in carbon footprint. (So if you're an airline, one answer to this challenge is to pursue your own heretical innovation and work toward fossil-fuel-free flying.)

10. **Find innovation partners.** Cash is tight, so scramble, scrimp, save, and do whatever you can to maintain R&D spending. Consider working with partners outside your industry, or even inside it, to solve common problems. Look for cross-sector initiatives like Sustainable Silicon Valley, a regional group trying to reduce carbon emissions. The organization is coordinating government, business, and community leaders in the San Francisco Bay area to develop a regional environmental plan, identify best practices and new ideas, and implement them.

When sharing won't do, consider buying your innovation, since it might be cheaper. A few companies—such as software giant Oracle—are using the downturn to pick up some small, innovative companies at bargain-basement prices. Others are finding and funding the garage innovators who are cash strapped in normal times and completely starved of capital today. A. G. Lafley, the CEO of Procter & Gamble, set a goal of sourcing 50 percent of new innovations from outside the company. P&G will then run new ideas through its impressive product development machine. Basically, the company invited the world into its innovation pipeline.

Green pressures and hard times require new solutions—it would be silly to believe your people have all the answers.

Think Big and Grab Share Now

The eleventh and overarching guideline is to think big, no matter your size. Small companies can lead the green innovation parade. In all the specific action areas in this book—from auxiliary power units for trucks to new software products that improve server utilization or map out your supply chain footprint—smaller companies are behind many of the most creative solutions. If you're a small or medium-size enterprise, green innovation is one place where you can plug into the green recovery.

Big or small, don't be bound by the tough times. Are you worried about saving money right now? Well, again, creativity is free. When you ask heretical questions, you push the boundaries. You may not end up where you thought, but it will be an improvement. As Ursula Burns from Xerox puts it, "If you shoot for a big goal and come up a little short, you still have something better than you did before."

If you think big enough about green innovation, it could guide your entire product portfolio and M&A strategies. Clorox, the cleaning products company, placed a green lens over its portfolio and made some sizable moves into new spaces. The company used a clever framework to think about the ways greener products would touch its customers' lives in three categories: products you eat or drink, products you put on your body, and products that go around you, such as household cleaners. It called this framework "in me, on me, around me."

Clorox's successful Brita water filter brand, which fills the "in me" category, is benefitting from a bottled water backlash. Customers who still want filtered water, but want to avoid the environmental downsides of the portable variety, can make their own. But the company didn't have a green product in the other two categories.

First, to fill the "on me" category, Clorox bought the fast-growing Burt's Bees and its line of natural personal care products. Then it launched the successful Green Works brand of cleaning products to fill the "around me" category.

Redefining your portfolio through a combination of in-house innovation and targeted purchases is an aggressive downturn strategy, but a smart one if you can pull it off.

All of the creative approaches in this chapter require the involvement of people from all over the company—innovators in product development, strategy and M&A, design, manufacturing, and many other departments can contribute to new thinking. Getting lean, smart, and creative requires everyone's buy-in and a deep understanding of your company's economic and environmental challenges and opportunities. Let's look now at how you can get your people engaged.

CHAPTER 5

Get (Your People) Engaged

Ray Anderson, the founder of sustainability leader Interface Inc., has said many times that a green focus rescued the company during tough times. Getting lean saved Interface hundreds of millions of dollars, which helped it survive the post-Internet-bubble downturn that hit the commercial flooring business hard. But another aspect of sustainability helped. As Anderson told an audience at the Rocky Mountain Institute, "In my fifty-two years in business, I've never seen an issue galvanize people in a company like sustainability."

Employees are the key to growth in good times and survival in bad. If they're on board, they can keep the company afloat and help it prepare for a stronger future. In these times of low morale, and perhaps *because* of the stress of harder economic conditions, many people want more meaning at work. A green focus will both engage and inspire your people to keep them going through tough times.

Because it helps you get lean, smart, and creative, green engagement will certainly have a large bottom-line impact on your business. But sometimes the pursuit of profit isn't enough. The environmental mission can give more meaning to many of the other initiatives in this book. Getting lean is moderately exciting, but people will be more motivated if they're doing it for the *dual* purposes of profit and environmental concern.

Let's go back to one idea from chapter 2, cutting back on travel. Erin Fitzgerald, the sustainability executive for the industry group Dairy Management Inc., says she hears many low-morale conversations in companies that sound like this: "Well, our expense budget has been cut, and we aren't flying anymore." It's depressing when framed that way. But, she asks, what if a company says instead, "We are going to reduce our environmental impacts this year and we are going to save money, so we'll fly less"? That, Fitzgerald says, is "a whole different conversation."

It's a great time to ask people to step up and take part in making the company a place that not only does the right thing but also thrives while doing it. The process may push people beyond their normal comfort zones. Addressing environmental challenges and opportunities requires a full value-chain perspective on the business; it's a far more extended view than most of us are used to. But new ways of thinking challenge and engage people.

Green issues also connect to personal lives much more than other strategic goals. It's natural to jump back and forth between thinking about reducing energy use to save money at home and getting lean to preserve capital at work.

There are clearly many ways to motivate employees, from incentives and pay to awards and recognition. But the point of this chapter is not to provide a tool kit for employee engagement. Instead, I'm making the case that to keep people engaged during hard times and get the most value out of green thinking, you'll need to accomplish two things:

1. Give employees a base of knowledge on environmental issues and their implications for the business.

2. Involve everyone in sustainability on multiple levels, both as workers and as people.

The end goal is to improve your company's performance and competitive position. But to do that, you need to get people engaged in the hard and rewarding work of greening your core business, your strategies, your operations, and your products and services. When your employees are more knowledgeable about and connected to environmental issues, your chances of getting there go way up.

But here's the best part for tight times: *engagement and behavior changes are close to free.* You're winning hearts and minds here. It might take some cajoling to fight inertia, but cash and capital outlays will be very small. As I prepared to write this book, I asked smart managers about where to look for quick efficiency wins in hard times. I heard repeatedly that the highest payback comes from people changes. This reality is why the Prius effect—the quick, noticeable reduction in energy use that occurs when people see real-time data—is so powerful. When managers have data on their performance, it engages them in the issue and stirs competitive juices. They often change their behavior without making any major capital investments.

To help your company survive tough times, you'll need people at all levels of the organization to share goals and a common understanding of the challenges and opportunities ahead.

Building a Foundation for Green Thinking: What Your People Should Know

One core idea in Jim Collins's groundbreaking book *Good to Great* is the importance of "facing the brutal facts." Through a powerful anecdote about prisoners of war, Collins makes the case that those who accept reality can survive the hard times and maintain hope for a better tomorrow. Those who rail against reality quite literally die.

In the business context, we face nothing but brutal facts right now. Economic downturns, declining sales, and squeezed profit margins are hard realities. Unfortunately, so are a few critical environmental truths. Resilient companies take in these new realities and change their products and services accordingly. The nimble may not only survive now, but emerge in a better competitive position later.

At all times, but especially today, doing business well is tough. Getting lean and smart is strategic and rewarding, but it can be hard work. Innovating and creating new products and services can be a lot of fun, but it's definitely not easy. So you want everyone to feel some passion, or at least deep understanding, about what you're trying to accomplish. Won't employees work harder if they understand *why* environmental challenges are real and *why* going green is good for business? When Shell CEO Jeroen van der Veer wrote a letter to shareholders in January 2008 and said plainly that dealing with climate change "will be hard work and there is little time," don't you think his employees appreciated the blunt honesty?

To put it more tactically, without some common understanding, your people may spin their wheels or not be engaged enough to spin them at all. Innovation efforts could miss the mark and spend scarce resources heading in the wrong direction. Efforts to reduce environmental impacts could focus on the wrong parts of the value chain or miss the best cost-savings opportunities. So the right training won't just focus on what employees do, but how they *think*.

What are these essential realities? Beyond the core idea that green is not a cost center, but a profitable path to growth (an underlying theme for this book), I'm talking about helping employees:

- Understand what climate change means for business (which is very different from everyone agreeing on the science).

- See the long-run constraints in natural resources and nonrenewable energy.

- View the business in the context of the full value chain, from suppliers to customers and beyond.

Some of these areas focus on belief systems, so it will require a sincere effort to move the needle on them. Throwing some basic information about environmental issues into internal training modules is not going to do it. Top executives will need to come out, and come out strong, with statements about the company's belief in environmental challenges and commitment to action.

The CEOs of some of the largest, most energy-intensive companies in the world have joined a group called the Climate Action Partnership. Members include GE, DuPont, Johnson & Johnson, PepsiCo, Deere, Duke Energy, and many others. In early 2007, and again in January 2009, the CEOs of some of these companies went to Washington, D.C., to ask for a federal cap on carbon emissions. Their presence sent a message to Congress. But more importantly, their actions made it clear to their own employees that they see environmental challenges as critical business issues. They demonstrated deep acceptance of the first of three key ideas to get your organization behind: climate change is a *business* challenge that's here to stay.

Understand That Climate Change Is a *Political* and *Business* Reality

I speak regularly to audiences of businesspeople with incredibly varied perspectives, politically, geographically, you name it. But on one topic, views are fairly consistent. I've asked audiences many times whether they believe scientists are in agreement on the basic findings on climate change (that is, it's real, and humans are causing it). In these informal polls, roughly 50 to 70 percent of businesspeople believe that significant disagreement remains within the scientific community.

On climate change, the reality is this: the scientists are in *vast* agreement. The Intergovernmental Panel on Climate Change (IPCC), the largest, broadest group of scientists ever assembled, declared climate change "unequivocal" in February 2007. But you don't have to agree with that consensus to recognize the reality that governments all over the world are moving forward based on the IPCC's findings. You also don't have to believe the science to see that most of the world's largest businesses have accepted the consensus enough to reduce their own emissions and demand the same of their partners. As the then CEO of Shell U.S., John Hofmeister, told the National Press Club in late 2006, "We have to deal with greenhouse gases . . . the debate is over."

Yet the average group of American businesspeople is not sure.

Now imagine a totally different scenario. It's Game 6 of the World Series, a tie game, bottom of the ninth inning. The lead-off hitter smacks the ball down the first base line. It goes over the fence, but just squeezes by the foul pole. It's a tough call, so the umps all gather, discuss their different perspectives, and agree—it was a home run. The game is over, tying the series. Fans, players, and commentators may debate, perhaps for years, whether the ball was really foul or fair. But they won't debate whether the umps actually made the call or whether the game was really over.

The fact that two-thirds of many business audiences still think that scientists don't agree is worrisome, for their companies and for the country. Businesses that ignore the overwhelming consensus to act on climate change will miss out on one of the most seismic shifts in government policy and business strategy in history. The companies that not only accept this fundamental reality, but innovate to profit from it, will have the advantage.

So educate your employees about global, national, and local regulations targeting carbon emissions. Share with them the demands from business customers and consumers for products and services that help them reduce their footprint. Use these facts to spur innovation.

> **The need to deal with climate change is not just a threat, it's a tremendous opportunity. Make sure employees understand *that* fact.**

Understand That Resources Are Not Infinite

As described in chapter 1, the resource and commodity supply crunch that's coming will be profound. It's a big mistake to operate as if any short-term commodity price collapse is a permanent state of affairs. Resource prices will remain volatile indefinitely, and they will most likely rise quickly when the upturn comes.

Many people have trouble swallowing the idea that the world is reaching some limits to growth. After all, the "we're running out of things" crowd has been wrong for at least 200 years, dating back to Thomas Malthus. But in March 2008, when the *Wall Street Journal* titled a long front-page article "New Limits to Growth Revive Malthusian Fears," something was clearly brewing. The argument against the limits-to-growth perspective has always been that we'll find new materials to replace those that get scarce and expensive. This time, the *Journal* said, "some of the resources now in great demand have no substitutes." The public pressure to cut back on fossil fuels, the demand for water, and rising standards of living for billions of people, the authors argued, will all strain resources for the foreseeable future.

But it's important to realize that we're facing limits to *traditional* expansion—growth based on fossil fuels and materials we need to dig up or cut down. All of that is a quantity issue. Our goal should be to maintain the growth of *quality* of life or of human potential. We're not talking about the old "put on a sweater to save energy" approach here (although, I have to ask why that's such a bad idea). Instead, we're trying to provide a high quality of living while using drastically less stuff. All of this change requires massive shifts in how we do business and how we use resources.

Employees need to see that the old ways will cost the company dearly, in good times or bad. Your business will need to get much more efficient (yes, leaner) with energy and materials, but employees may not feel the pressure to make that happen if they don't understand the core problem.

There's a macro, national-level argument here as well, one that will appeal to employees in their roles as citizens. When the country's mood is dark, speaking of a higher calling may help keep spirits up. Just communicate to employees that relying on resources, often from parts of the world that don't like us very much, is a security threat, for both countries and companies.

Basic resource constraints are brutal facts. But you can use these facts to engage people and help them understand *why* getting lean is crucial to your company's profitability. You can use tough realities to guide innovation toward solutions that help build a more secure company and world.

See the Value in the Value Chain

In most industries, the biggest part of a company's environmental footprint falls outside its direct control. For energy-using products, such as electronics or cars, the energy consumed during the use phase outweighs the emissions in manufacturing or the supply chain. In other industries, such as food and agriculture, it's the upstream impacts in the supply chain that matter most. For dairy or meat products, the methane produced by livestock dominates the carbon footprint (as one dairy company executive told me, succinctly, "our risk is the cow").

Influencing things out of your direct control is a challenge at any time. Asking suppliers to go green when times are harder seems unlikely to work. But if your sourcing managers understand the benefits of value-chain thinking and how your suppliers can save money by getting leaner and greener, the conversation may go better. For industries where the footprint is primarily downstream, there's a real opportunity to help customers reduce those impacts. If you can make the case that your products or services lower their environmental costs, you may actually gain customers in hard times.

But here's another important reason to teach a value chain perspective: mitigating possible business-threatening risks. In these tight times, any additional unexpected blow to an already tenuous business could tip the scales the wrong way. In 2007, Mattel discovered lead in its toys and conducted an expensive recall. Imagine if this kind of brand-destroying disaster hit your company when profits were already thin. Surviving economic uncertainty may hinge not only on conserving cash and cutting costs, but also on asking employees to identify hidden risks throughout the value chain.

Teaching employees about the realities, risks, and opportunities stemming from climate change, resource constraints, and value chains can help bring on a green recovery. But truly building a greener culture will require engaging employees as workers *and* people.

Engaging Employees on Multiple Levels: Sustainability at Home and Work

During times of low morale, a sustainability focus can engage people in new ways. Many companies are asking their people to think about their environmental impacts in three distinct areas:

1. Their personal lives

2. Around the office

3. The business itself, including the full value chain of products and services

The first two areas represent important starting points. Helping employees get lean at home shows them the benefits of green thinking in a personal way, especially when cash is tight. And letting employees fix symbolic eco-waste at the office (such as moving to two-sided copying) can ease the mental transition to making larger changes in how the company operates. The trick is not to let any excitement around green go to waste, especially when companies need new ideas and full involvement to survive tough times.

Greening Their Lives

Wal-Mart's Personal Sustainability Project is the mother of all sustainability engagement programs. More than 500,000 employees have signed up for this voluntary program and made a commitment to health or planet, from quitting smoking to biking to work. Many companies have talked about sustainability in personal terms for years, usually around Earth Day when they ask employees to plant trees. But Wal-Mart and some other dedicated companies are putting more structure around these programs.

Some are throwing in money and perks to encourage people to take action in their personal lives. Insurance giant Swiss Re set up a fund for employees who make "environmentally friendly investments" at home, such as buying hybrid cars or rooftop solar panels. The company's "CO You2" program provides up to $4,500 to employees for these green expenditures and demonstrates Swiss Re's commitment to reducing carbon emissions.

The total investment in this kind of program can be fairly small given the incredible good will generated with employees who want to save money at home. But even if capital is tight, smaller perks, such as giving hybrid drivers up-front parking or helping a little with public transportation costs, can go a long way. Granted, these are minor gestures, but they matter in times of low morale.

Greening the Office

Cisco CEO John Chambers holds a large, monthly "birthday breakfast" for employees (about one-twelfth at a time, I presume). One month, Chambers focused his opening remarks on the company's green efforts. When he opened up the floor to questions, the first person did not ask about Cisco's commitment to reduce its own air travel, or its teleconferencing products that help others do the same, or even the energy use of all the millions of routers out there. No, the employee in question just wanted to know, "Why are we still using plastic water bottles around the office?"

Lucky for Chambers, he had an answer—the company was already planning to switch to filtered water. Many companies are addressing these opportunities for greening the office, usually focusing on day-to-day water and paper use. A friend of mine is the programming director for a national cable channel. Every week, the network's production and marketing teams meet to discuss upcoming shows. Until recently, they printed out PowerPoint decks of twenty to thirty pages for each show—for forty people. They were using up to 7,000 pages a week and roughly 650 reams of paper a year, all for information that had no use past that meeting. So the team decided to go paperless—they now display each slide deck on a wide-screen TV everyone can see.

Many organizations are forming "green teams" of employees to find and tackle these kinds of issues. These self-motivated groups are a particularly good idea for small and medium-size enterprises that don't have a dedicated environmental organization. At companies of all sizes, the employee teams usually need support. To help green team members collaborate, Boeing is using a range of online instruments such as blogs, FAQs, and wikis (the online communities like Wikipedia that are sources of information edited by everyone). These social media tools also help the organization gather intelligence from the people much closer to the company's challenges and opportunities than management. As Applied Materials' Bruce Klafter says, "It's really important to *listen* to employees, particularly in large, diverse, multicultural companies. Employees usually know what's going on much sooner and with greater detail than any executive or support group (like EH&S) will."

Even with help, these mostly self-directed teams tend to focus somewhat narrowly, often setting out to eliminate relatively minor environmental problems like water bottles in the cafeteria (which apparently really annoy people). But giving employees an outlet to make changes can be a good morale booster in hard times, and it can form a launching pad for thinking about larger issues that tie more directly to profitability.

Greening the Business

Clearly, the greatest value lies in getting employees to improve the business itself. In hard times in particular, companies need to encourage everyone to turn their green focus onto the company. Personal Sustainability Projects (PSPs) can give people a fuller understanding of their footprints as workers, family members, and people. But imagine what it could mean to the business to turn that energy inward.

One story from Wal-Mart demonstrates the potential. For his PSP commitment, one finance manager chose to reduce waste at home. He started by recycling more carefully and trying to see how little garbage he could end up with in his trash can each week. As he got more passionate about the topic, he joined a sustainability network focused on waste at work. He brought his financial skills to bear and crafted some ROI calculations to prove how lucrative many of Wal-Mart's current and potential waste-reduction projects were. Thus the engagement on the personal level drove him to create value for the company. But you can't just wait for this virtuous circle to happen. It's now time to push employees to make the connections.

The same applies to the green team activities. We need to harness these nascent networks immediately to help companies get lean in tight times. Double-sided copying and eliminating water bottles are important, symbolic changes, but it's time to force an evolution. Ask your employees to focus team efforts on innovating to reduce energy use or to design new products that satisfy green-minded customers. Green teams, if used right, can morph from mainly engagement tools to something even more fundamentally valuable to the business.

Unfortunately, the number of companies leveraging bottom-up creativity and knowledge to generate business-wide green improvements is small. But one recent, powerful example demonstrates how to use training on key principles, and engagement more broadly, to improve the business today and prepare for better times tomorrow. Even though this is not a purely green example, we can learn something important about engagement.

Despite the success of models like the Prius, Toyota has not been immune to the unprecedented collapse of sales in the auto industry. But it has taken a different approach to its workers than others in the industry. Instead of laying them off or sending idle workers home to collect a paycheck, Toyota decided to increase training on car-building skills and on core Toyota principles and philosophies, such as lean manufacturing. One assembly worker from Indiana, Bob Mason, told the *Wall Street Journal* in late 2008 how grateful the employees are that Toyota "thought enough of us to keep us here."

How loyal will Mason and other Toyota employees be? How hard will they work to improve their skills and the results of the company? The *Journal* also reported that management "hopes to extract . . . better quality and productivity when production resumes." Isn't it more likely now that Toyota will see exactly that result and pull even further ahead of competitors?

Imagine taking Toyota's example and training people on the core green principles, ideas, and tactics laid out in this book. You can engage employees in practices that create significant value for the business quickly (which will keep CFOs and environmental skeptics happy), but also connect them to a larger purpose. Increasing training in these tough times seems like a luxury, but it may save your company.

By getting lean on stuff, not on people, you earn incredible loyalty. Generating excitement around new, green ways of doing business, finding ways to use less energy and materials, and creating products and services that help customers reduce *their* environmental impacts will keep your people going in hard times and drive profitability.

Ownership and Alignment

One final thought on employee engagement. On top of building a base of knowledge and connecting with people on multiple levels, it's important to give people ownership of environmental goals and the tools to act on them. Incentives, awards, and all the other ways you normally move people in an organization still apply. Pat Tiernan, a longtime tech industry exec who was vice president of sustainability at HP, says that the best way to engage people in green is to "show the relevance to, and alignment with, core business goals . . . make it integral to their success, and they come along much more willingly."

One of the best tools for demonstrating that alignment is hard data, so I come back to getting smart. Office Depot has developed effective environmental metrics for all major aspects of the business. The company's sustainability report includes a table that shows how the business is tracking against three broad, simply stated goals:

- Increasingly buy green, which is about upstream issues in procurement and supply chains

- Increasingly be green, which covers company operations

- Increasingly sell green, which gets at the quantity of environmentally preferable products sold to customers (a downstream view)

The goals demonstrate an admirable value-chain perspective, but the best part of the table is the column that lists, by title, a "functional owner" for every metric. With this tool, Office Depot makes individual executives accountable for pieces of the story. For example, the vice president in charge of logistics and transportation can see data on the amount of fuel used to deliver products, the carbon dioxide per delivery, and so on. The head of operations can see a metric like "ratio of cost of waste to revenue from recycling." (So if the company wants to turn waste from a cost to a profit center, that metric would have to fall below 1.0, which it hasn't quite yet.) But more importantly, the metrics on how each function is doing on environmental goals, especially ones that tie directly to fiscal results, are out there for everyone to see. And everyone knows who's responsible for performance, good or bad.

The leading companies are making the connection between performance on sustainability issues and your career development. Mike Duke, CEO of Wal-Mart, in the speech he gave right before taking over the job in February 2009, said that he wanted every employee involved in the mission. But he went further and declared, "The leaders that get ahead in Wal-Mart will be ones that demonstrate their commitment to sustainability . . . you won't be viewed in the same way if you put this on the back burner."

Eventually, green will be a part of everyone's job— just a normal part of doing business in every function, from C-level executives to product designers to marketing and finance managers. For now, it's critical to send the message that the company is serious about green issues, and then provide access to the knowledge and tools employees need to understand these challenges.

You'll build a culture of authentic commitment to sustainability, which will excite your people like nothing you've ever seen. Consider sustainability an essential tool for attracting the best people, and then keeping everyone engaged through good times and bad. Once on board, these excited employees will help create stronger companies that will not only survive uncertain economic climates, but also prosper as times get better.

Conclusion
Survival, Relevance, and Advantage

In tough economic times, we're all faced with hard choices about how to allocate scarce resources. It may seem as if you can't tackle everything this book suggests all at once. You might think that looking for opportunities to get lean sounds good, but all that data collection, engagement, and innovation work can wait. A more limited approach will certainly yield *some* benefits, but you'd miss the game-changing opportunity.

These four paths to a green recovery reinforce each other, so you'll get the most value out of acting on *all* of them. As you can see in my green recovery framework (see figure that follows), getting smart and getting engaged provide the underpinning for the more tangible

The green recovery framework

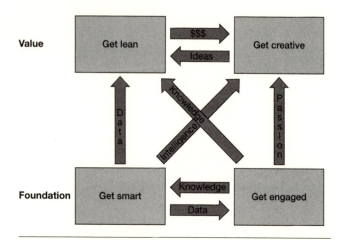

value creation from getting lean and getting creative. In that sense, the foundation areas need to move first and fastest (although all should move at once).

Look at "get smart" and the support it provides the others. Collecting better data on your footprint helps you identify ways to get lean and shows your employees where the true opportunities are, which can help fire them up. Getting smart also fuels and focuses creativity by providing critical market intelligence about the value chain and where the opportunities in your industry might be.

Turning to "get engaged," when you truly excite your people, they bring passion to creative endeavors, the manpower and perspective to help with data collection, and broad knowledge about the business and where the company can get lean.

Finally, look at the mutually beneficial relationship between "get lean" and "get creative." Getting lean frees up money to fund innovation, and at the same time, creativity is crucial for finding new ways to get much more efficient—a powerful virtuous circle. When your company is doing all of these things in sync, you create value much faster.

One example from Burt's Bees, a leader in natural personal care products and one of the most sustainability-focused companies around, demonstrates how all of these concepts work together. Everyone at Burt's Bees is engaged in the mission and understands the benefits of environmental thinking. They seek out data on their environmental impacts whenever possible. Recently, the operations managers were looking for ways to get lean and used energy meters to conduct a "microscopic analysis of energy use" in manufacturing. Since the meters cost just a few hundred dollars, getting smart was pretty cheap.

The data highlighted one specific area of high energy use. In the lip balm production line, they were using PVC plastic to create a tamper-evident shrink wrap. They used considerable energy to heat the plastic to cover the product (shaped like the classic ChapStick tube). As CEO John Replogle told me, "It was lose-lose-lose. For consumers, they were a pain to open, PVC is nasty stuff environmentally, and it cost us money because we used a ton of energy and slowed down the production line."

So designers and production managers got creative. By simply extending the branded paper wrapping that was already on the tube by a quarter of an inch and perforating it, they completely eliminated the need for the plastic— and the energy to heat it. Now customers open the lip balm by just turning the cap to break the perforated paper seal. This single innovation has sped up production and slashed energy use on that line by 42 percent.

The change—from data collection to product re-design to streamlining production—took less than six months. Burt's Bees is rolling this idea out to twenty-five other products and has cut PVC use and costs by 90 percent. The soft benefits are harder to measure but also real. The product annoys customers less, fits with the company's mission and brand better, and as Replogle says, "allows us to talk to Wal-Mart and others about our sustainability packaging." It's a great win for the company, its retail partners, and its consumers.

This kind of innovation obviously saves money—in this case hundreds of thousands of dollars. But more importantly, it creates a ripple of benefits, making the company permanently leaner, faster, and less costly to operate. Tom Fitz, the vice president of sustainable engineering (a title that tells you something about the culture of the place), comments that "there's a misconception that sustainability costs a lot of money. But so many wins come from changes in processes and behaviors. The rewards are not only financial savings, but the benefits of having a better infrastructure that's more nimble and ready for the future."

Becoming a leaner, more innovative enterprise will help you save money now and keep your customers and employees happy. A more environmentally savvy culture and company will also have the advantage when times get better and the green wave gathers even more strength. You will be better prepared to answer powerful stakeholders who will demand more and more of you. In fact, in an environmentally sensitive world, going green may be the only path to survival.

Survival

Economic recessions are life-and-death situations for countless organizations. Those that endure today would be wise to consider what other crises might come in the future, and how they will survive those. As hard as it may be to imagine, green pressures will force even larger, more sustained changes in business than current economic pressures. We're talking about a fundamental shift in how the world works. We're changing how business operates to deal with resource constraints and much higher demands from customers, employees, and governments around the world.

Those that are unprepared for this new way of doing business may not make it. As sustainability consultant Will Sarni says, "When we come out the other side of this, the U.S. will have an energy and carbon policy, and maybe even a policy addressing water. This brave new world will kill companies that view environmental sustainability as a side issue."

One sector in particular, the U.S. auto industry, has already demonstrated the dangers of ignoring green pressures. Some commentators suggest that Detroit's troubles stem from higher labor, health-care, and pension costs. True, but those factors affect profitability, not necessarily demand. Another argument made by automakers themselves is that their downfall stemmed from the credit crunch. Yes, the financial meltdown sealed their fate, but the declining health of these American icons was already in the cards. Months before the financial catastrophe of late 2008, energy prices rose fast, and GM, Ford, and Chrysler were in very bad trouble.

Look at the brutal facts on U.S. auto sales during the first eight months of 2008 (see figure). When consumers began demanding smaller, more energy-efficient cars, the companies with greener fleets—basically the Japanese automakers—fared pretty well. When the green wave of energy resource constraints caused energy prices to spike, Detroit was not ready.

Sales for the former Big Three were down 15 to 25 percent during that crucial time, while the companies with

U.S. auto sales, first 8 months of 2008 vs. 2007

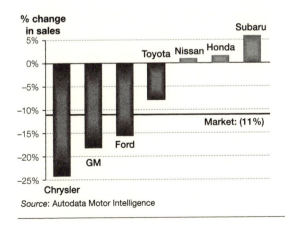

Source: Autodata Motor Intelligence

greener fleets actually saw sales rise. Interestingly, Toyota, one of the green business leaders, hit some hard times as well, but not because its energy-efficient product line was failing—the Prius was still dominating hybrid sales and flying off lots. But Toyota had pursued a big-vehicle strategy more aggressively than the other Japanese automakers, and it got caught in the same whirlpool as Detroit. But sales at Nissan, Honda, and Subaru rose for the first eight months of 2008, and Subaru managed to end the entire year up—a major victory when the whole market was down 18 percent for the year.

U.S. car companies missed the green wave in a profound way. It's an American business tragedy, but denying the core reasons for the failure won't help anyone. Other industries can learn from this example and avoid the same fate. If your business or your products rely heavily on energy and other natural resources, you may be at great risk. When better times come and energy prices rise again, the leanest companies will be in a much better position to thrive. Inefficient companies that are fossil fuel dependent anywhere in their value chain will struggle.

The risks of inaction are high, but looking forward, the upside from getting lean, smart, creative, and engaged is even greater. While Detroit faltered, Subaru's sales *grew* during one of the worst auto industry downturns in history, and Toyota ascended to the title of the world's largest auto company. Remember the *Fortune* magazine comment on how the lead can change hands during the uphill portions of a race? Well, the auto industry hit a monumentally steep incline, and Toyota's hybrid gas-electric engine overpowered all the V-8s Detroit could throw at it.

But the benefits of a green-themed recovery are even deeper than sales and growth—they make sure your company stays relevant to the times.

Relevance

If it seems as if Wal-Mart has appeared frequently in this book, it's for good reason. No company in the world is pushing the sustainability agenda at such scale—or as relentlessly onto others. The company's pressure on supply chains from China to Chattanooga is reshaping industries. Wal-Mart has profoundly influenced value chains for years, but this time it's in the service of reducing waste, slashing energy use, and saving money by using green strategies.

Wal-Mart is now taking a more philosophical, strategic, and long-term view on how to stay vibrant and important to customers. One top executive made a fascinating observation at the company's big sustainability meeting in Beijing in late 2008. For a hundred years, one retailer has dominated the U.S. market—but only one at a time and only for about a generation (think of Woolworth's or Sears). Wal-Mart is today's leader, but how will it stay on top? Will the children of today's Wal-Mart shoppers still want the company in their communities, and will they shop there? It seems likely that the retail giant will stay in society's good graces only if it satisfies the evolving demands of its customers.

One of Wal-Mart's sustainability execs, Rand Waddoups, put it to me this way: "Sustainability makes us a more efficient and relevant business. The efficiency helps lower our costs, which we can pass on to customers in the form of low prices." For now, getting lean, smart, and creative will help the company keep its low-price promise. In the longer run, innovation in Wal-Mart's supply chain to produce more sustainable products will help the company stay relevant. With consumers redefining quality to include environmental and social criteria, Wal-Mart *must* become sustainable, or it will eventually fade away.

I would argue that Wal-Mart faces an even larger existential challenge: can the core business model—selling inexpensive products sourced from all over the world—ever be sustainable? Put another way, are the retail giants and our collective consumption habits sustainable? Perhaps not, but as green pressures rise, these questions become the thorniest and most relevant of all. Pursuing sustainability in all aspects of the business will help Wal-Mart, and all of us, find some answers.

Look at some of the other companies I've discussed in this book and how *their* actions keep them relevant. Toyota and Honda gave car buyers what they needed when energy prices peaked. Hospitality companies like IHG or consumer product companies like P&G stay current by making their products and services more energy efficient and less toxic. Tennant's floor-cleaning breakthrough redefines relevance in its market by satisfying customers in new ways.

When both HP and Xerox work to shrink the footprint of ink, or even reduce the number of devices their customers buy, it may seem to threaten parts of their business, but they are actually evolving to stay relevant. When Waste Management helps clients produce *less* waste (which they normally get paid for by quantity), doesn't that make the company more relevant during tight times? Those companies that eat their own lunch before someone else does can avoid becoming completely *ir*relevant—and they often discover new efficiencies or revenue streams in the process.

The status quo for companies that don't adopt core green principles will not be steady performance, but declining financial results and loss of share of shelves and minds. Ensuring relevance will require an investment of time and resources. But remember, *investments are not costs,* especially if you're enabling future growth. If companies like Wal-Mart, Waste Management, Xerox, HP, Toyota, Honda, P&G, Clorox, and many others stay relevant, they will do so by helping create a sustainable economy. And they will have the edge over those that don't evolve.

Growth and Competitive Advantage

It's very easy to focus too much on today's pressing needs and lose sight of the bigger picture. Those who don't continue to improve their businesses and innovate, even in tight times, will fall farther behind.

The steps you need to take to succeed in a greener world long term also help in the short run—and vice versa. Getting lean today saves money, but truly pays off as you permanently lower your cost of doing business and bullet-proof yourself from rising energy prices. Getting smart means knowing your business better than ever before, allowing you to target the quick wins with the largest paybacks and identify big risks and opportunities before your competitors do. Getting creative about how you operate can save money now and help you leapfrog your competition to satisfy customers in leaner, greener ways over time. Finally, you won't be able to do any of this unless you engage your people and get them going in the same direction.

For today and tomorrow, and *especially* during uncertain times, pursuing a green recovery will make your business more competitive. As Burt's Bees' Replogle says,

> *It's counterintuitive, but now is the time to accelerate our commitment to sustainability. Why? The trends that made green hot before we went into this [downturn] will become the norm in the near future. In a few years, green will be a competitive requirement. And if your competition is pulling back, you can use that competitive requirement to gain competitive advantage.*

Even while companies fight their way through the economic challenges today, the world is still evolving. Standards for environmental performance, transparency, and social responsibility are rising. Those who get to this new world first will help define it.

So push the boundaries and ask those heretical questions about how your industry works today or how it might satisfy customers in the greenest way possible. Be the leanest and smartest, but also create a culture of creativity where everyone is fully engaged in the larger mission.

If you do these things, you'll build an organization that's sustainable in every sense of the word. You'll survive today's travails, thrive as things get better, and emerge from the downturn on top. In the process, you'll redefine your business and help build a leaner, greener world.

Acknowledgments

Any book is impossible to write without the contributions of many talented people—especially a book that's trying to reflect a current reality. I could in no way have accomplished this without reaching out to some very knowledgeable executives and managers who graciously spent time giving me new perspectives, stories, and ideas. Without all of you, this book would be much poorer. Thank you to Karen Arena, Ann Bamesberger, Subodh Bapat, Christian Belady, Rob Bernard, Phil Berry, Patrick Blair, Ursula Burns, Jim Butcher, Jodie Cadieux, Patty Calkins, Yola Carlough, Seetha Coleman-Kammula, Dave Douglas, Tyler Elm, Alyssa Farrell, Tom Fitz, Erin Fitzgerald, Elizabeth Fretheim, Jeff Goodell, Edward Gromos, Mark Helms, Laura Ipsen, Jeremy Jaech, David Jerome, Eileen Kersul, Chris Killingstad, Bruce Klafter, Michelle

Lapinski, Joyce LaValle, Andy Leventhal, Kate Lister, Dr. Mingsheng Liu, Peggy Liu, Kathryn Lovik, Kory Lundberg, Diana Lyon, Nicole Maloney, Brandi McManus, Doug McMillon, Scott McNealy, Erin McQuade, Stan Mierzejewski, Terry Mutter, Dean Nelson, Steve Newcomb, Frank O'Brien-Bernini, Jackie Ogden, Heidi Pate, Melissa Perlman, John Replogle, Dawn Rittenhouse, Len Sauers, Yalmaz Siddiqui, Paul Snyder, David Steiner, Beth Stevens, Jana Thompson, Pat Tiernan, Andrew Van Der Laan, Joe Vivinetto, Rand Waddoups, Frances Way, and Duane Woods.

I also want to thank some other big thinkers who have inspired me in my career. These people know a great deal about business and/or the environment. Some wrote the books that made me change careers a decade ago, some taught me new things about this evolving space, and some have become sounding boards for my wacky ideas. I'm lucky enough to call many of them colleagues or friends now. Thanks to Ray Anderson, Scott Anthony, Janine Benyus, Jim Collins, John Elkington, Dan Esty, Thomas Friedman, Paul Hawken, Gary Hirshberg, Amory Lovins, Hunter Lovins, Joel Makower, Jacquie Ottman, C. K. Prahalad, Will Sarni, Andrew Shapiro, James Gustave Speth, Joseph Stanislaw, and Adam Werbach.

This book was also supported by research that needed to be done in days, not weeks. I reached out to Katie Kross from the Center for Sustainable Enterprise at the University of North Carolina's Kenan-Flagler Business School. She sent me two wonderful research assistants, Peter Gallo and Brandon Little. Thank you both for your quick efforts to find the best data and resources and for helping to make sure the details were right.

The research for this book was made much easier by the existence of a few green-themed content providers online. These news and information companies have made it their missions to collect sustainability stories and make them easy to find. So thanks to the people behind sites such as environmentalleader.com, greenbiz.com, and of course sustainablelifemedia.com (SLM), my content partner for my monthly strategy e-letter. A special thank-you to the whole SLM team, and KoAnn Skrzyniarz and Emily Cowan in particular, for giving me an outlet for my writing and providing deep backup for my research.

I want to thank also two readers who always make the time for me and make my work better. To Matt Blumberg, who has read more books than humanly possible, thank you for your insightful comments about what a business book should look and feel like. To Professor

Marian Chertow, thank you for making sure the green business side of the book is fundamentally sound.

To the team at Harvard Business Press, thank you so much for all your intellectual brainpower about what would make this book work, and for your ongoing efforts to make sure as many people as possible see it. Thanks to Todd Berman, Erin Brown, Stephani Finks, Audra Longert, Michelle Morgan, Jacque Murphy, and Jen Waring. A special thank you to my editor Ania Wieckowski for keeping the book on course, and for incredibly cogent and helpful edits, all done very fast. Most importantly, I sincerely thank my editor Paul Michelman, the man who brought the core idea for *Green Recovery* to me in the first place. Any omissions in this book are my own, but anything that works, Paul had a hand in. To Paul I say, this is all your fault.

My family has been unbelievably supportive of my work in general and my crazy hours while writing this book. My business is a family affair: my mother, Gail, runs my back office; and my father, Jan, after a successful career in business, has provided constant feedback as my chief strategist and adviser. Finally, to my wife, Christine, I can't thank her enough (although she's bound to make me try). She has been a rock during this whirlwind writing process. She made sure our two boys, Joshua and

Jacob, stayed healthy and happy as she always does, but she really took on the full parenting load while I was stuck inside my own head. More than that, as an experienced corporate executive and intellectual partner, she read every word multiple times and made the book much better. I am lucky enough to make my living doing what I love, and Christine enables me to do it.

Thank you to all who have helped make this happen.

Index

Index

Index

Index

Index

Index

About the Author

Andrew Winston is a globally recognized expert on green business and advises some of the world's leading companies on how to profit from environmental thinking. His clients have included Bank of America, Bayer, Boeing, HP, and PepsiCo. Andrew is the coauthor of the bestseller, *Green to Gold*; writes a weekly column on strategy for Harvard Business Online; and appears frequently in major national media outlets such as the *New York Times, Wall Street Journal*, and *Business Week*.

Andrew is also a highly respected and sought-after corporate speaker, reaching large audiences around the world. His talks combine passion and practicality into an entertaining, up-to-date, and strategic review of the greening of business and society. Andrew's earlier career included corporate strategy work at the Boston Consulting Group and management positions in marketing and business development at Time Warner and MTV. He received his BA in Economics from Princeton, an MBA from Columbia, and a Masters of Environmental Management from Yale. He lives in Riverside, CT with his wife and two young sons.

To connect with Andrew, follow his blog and other writings, and to find out more about him, please visit www.andrewwinston. com.